# Ancient Indian Civilizations and Dynasties

By

Dr. M. L. Babu

Sham S. Misri

Kusum Babu

1

Contents

# PREFACE

The purpose of this monogram is not to write the history of India and its civilizations. The sole aim of this write up is to introduce the reader to ancient India, its Monarchs, Vedic civilization and its contribution to world. Out of all civilizations, this one is most neglected. This civilization and its contribution is grossly ignored by contemporary history books.

India should have occupied a significant space in world history. Instead it finds its name in foot notes of world history. In fact, India has been cradle of human civilization and founder of scientific ideas.

Philosophy of India rose as an enquiry in to mystery of Life and Existence.

As an off shoot, this monogram clears the notion of Aryan invasion of India in 1500BC, a myth created by west to legitimize their rule of India as well to down grade the indigenous advanced civilization.

I am thankful to my wife Kusum for inspiring me to write this monogram. I am thankful to Parum Misri and Sumeet Misri for their help.

It is because of their diligence in copy editing, cover design and other useful inputs that this monogram has been possible. Thankful to Julish Bhat for his assistance.

Finally, I dedicate this monogram to youth of India who should be proud of their heritage unlike their elders who have been skeptical about India's past.

Dr. M. L. Babu

# INTRODUCTION

The theory of the Aryan migration into India from somewhere has been so often repeated by the Western scholars that it has become an article of faith even with the Indian scholars!

"In the days when historian supposed that history had begun with Greece, Europe gladly believed that India has been a hotbed of barbarism and savagery."

In 1924 the world of scholarship was again roused by news from India. Sir John Marshall announced that he had discovered at Mohenjo-Daro, on the western bank of the Lower Indus, remains of what seemed to be an older civilization than any yet known to historians. The Indications are that Mohenjo-Daro was at its height when Cheops built the first great pyramid; that it had commercial, religious, and artistic connections with Samaria, and Babylonia. It survived over 3000 years, until the third century before Christ. [1]

When Sir Marshall saw Indus relics in Mohenjo-Daro and Harappa; Indian civilization had a quantum jump from a few hundred BC to 3000 BC. Then came many other scholars both Indian and foreign who came to conclusion that India had a mighty civilization in past. Max Muller, after compiling Vedas wrote, "If you ask me which country reached its glory first, I will point to India. " Same scholar had earlier said that India had no worthy civilization in past. With satellite Imaging, new excavations and other finds one becomes reasonably certain that India had a distinct culture of its own in past. Continued religious practices in present India give added Credence to India's glorious past.

Since the nineteenth century, India's ancient history from Vedic times and the true content of the Veda have both been distorted by a narrow-minded and indifferent scholarship. British rulers, European scholars and missionaries combined in a campaign to mock the roots of Indian Civilization, and used the wholly groundless Aryan Invasion theory to sow seeds of division in the Indian society - "divide and rule. " It was also "to divide and convert."

The same fallacies continue to be promoted today. Unfortunately, many of the wounds the Aryan Invasion theory inflicted on Indian society are still painfully open today, nurtured by politicians, who have made sure that divisions between castes have been sharpening rather than subsiding - for the simple reason that without such divisions they would all be out of business. Today, it is necessary to examine the birth of the Aryan myth, and the misuses it has bred; it then gives a fresh look at the invasion theory in the light of recent scientific evidence, and shows how it now stands overwhelmingly disproved[2]. All western writers tried to claim to get inspiration from Greek philosophy. Then they went on to Say that Indians got inspiration through Greece to develop their own philosophies. This they say despite their being enough evidence that Indian philosophies had taken definite shape around 800BC—1000BC.

It is extremely difficult to decipher India's past due to many things. Firstly, we have to dig too much of the past about which we which have scanty literature available today. Most of the literature of ancient India is either lost with time or was deliberately destroyed by foreigners. Ancient Indians knew value of history but they had less means to protect their monograms. Secondly, they were inclusive. They kept whatever they knew a closely guarded secret. Little they realized that their way of transmission of secrets orally will be lost to future generations. Writing of literature started very late [500BC—1000BC], by this time most of its glory was already lost. Hence the literature which came up was a mix up, where facts were woven with author's dispensation. It needs a real scholar, to get to real essence out of this confusing literature. It is this confusion in literature which has been exploited by western writers and they started telling no worthy Civilization existed in India in ancient times. They were joined in this by a handful of Indians who had no deep knowledge about Sanskrit.

It has now become a myth that Aryans migrated to India in 1500BC. Evidence is accumulating day by day that Aryans were Indians who migrated to Iran and west from India. There are writers who opine now that Indus civilization is post Vedic. Indologists who invented Aryan invasion theory postulated that Rigveda was written in 250BC but later fixed its date much earlier.

It is clear that India had a culture long before other civilizations came on earth. Vayu Purana mentions about ancient history of Bharata [India]. Suta wrote Puranas. The Puranas in Present form have been compiled very late [Gupta period]. Pargiter[3] believes oldest Puranas were written at the time of Vedic texts. Traditional history has its value and it is possible that old faith and its philosophy was chiefly a way of life. Slowly a rigid religion developed with all its rituals and ceremonies which we now call **Hinduism**. Professor Winternitz[4] thinks that beginning of Vedic literature goes back to 2000BC----2500BC. Many believe Rig-Veda was written around 1500BC. Looking at scriptures which are a product of human mind we have to remember the age in which they were written and the vast distance in time and thought which separates it from us.

Professor MacDonnell[5] says importance of Indian literature lies in its originality. Rigidity in caste factor led to loss in creativity and decline of race. A mix of free thought and Orthodoxy lived side by side. An appeal was always made to ancient authorities but little attempt was made to interpret their truth. Net result was decline of India.

Plotinus studied Iranian and Indian philosophy and was influenced by the mystic elements in Upanishads. From Plotinus many of these ideas are said to have gone to St Augustine and through him influenced the Christianity of the day. Max Muller, Schopenhauer and others have sung praises of Upanishads. In them, they felt joy! A cry came out; human thought seemed to have reached its very peak. Indian culture cannot be well understood if mythology is totally taken away and ignored. It becomes inarticulate. Mythology adds cover to the fruit it has preserved till today. It also held multicolored society divided in many ways in harmony and giving them common background of traditions and ethical life. Mythology is seen in every religion and nationalism everywhere has clouded the underlying truth.

Ancient India started with amalgamation of Aryan, Dravidian and some aboriginals. Stress was laid on life to make it comfortable. The Concept of God and metaphysics are late developments.

Manu gave law to country. What the Indians were like is difficult to conceive but a vague picture can be made out. They were lighthearted race, confident and proud of their traditions, dabbling in search for the mysterious, full of questions addressed to nature and human life, attaching importance to the standards and values they had created, but taking life easily and joyously. Such was then ancient India where search for truth gave it vitality; mythology gave it mobility which carried it till today. It may be mentioned here that Idol worship is not Vedic. It was introduced in India in post Buddha period because Buddhist followers worshiped his image. Staunch Hindu's made images [Idols] to make masses understand invisible which was criticized by Lord Buddha. Caste, an Aryan creation had totally different meaning then. Vedic teaching strongly believes in Karma [you are recognized by your work and not by birth]. Caste system was a manipulation to dominate society. There are innumerable examples of Shudras becoming Brahmins in Vedic age. Ultimately this Brahaminic greed for power and rigidity of caste system led to fall of India.

# PRE –HISTORIC INDIA

Earth formed about 4. 54 billion years back. It was initially molten, eventually outer layer of Planet cooled to form solid crest. As it started reshaping continents broke and fell apart.

Around 180million years back continent Pangaea broke apart. By the end of Mesozoic era the continents had drifted into present form. Laurasia became North America and Eurasia while Gondwana spilt Into South America, Africa, Australia, Antarctica and Indian subcontinent. It collided with Asian Plate and this impact gave rise to Himalayas.

History of India begins with evidence of human activity as long as 75000 years ago or with earlier hominid H. Erectus from about 500, 000 years ago. Earliest modern human fossil, Narmada man is dated 250, 000 back, found in Gujarat. There is also an indication that India might have been inhabited somewhere 500, 000 years to 200, 000 years ago. Tool crafted by Protohumans that have been dated back to 2Million years, have been discovered in North West India. The earliest archeological site in the subcontinent is the

Paleolithic site in Soan River Valley[6]. In Neolithic period more extensive settlement of the subcontinent occurred approximately 12000 years ago. First confirmed semi-permanent settlements have been seen in Bhimbetka rock shelters in modern Madhya Pradesh. Early Neolithic period is represented by Bhirrana findings [7500BC] in Haryana, Mehargarh [7000BC—9000BC] in Baluchistan[7.]

Agriculture sprang up in 5000BC[8]. Urbanization occurred with Indus valley civilization.

*Racial types in prehistoric India:*

The most plausible theory seems to be that long before the supposed Aryan invasion, the Indian Subcontinent was inhabited by diverse groups of peoples who migrated from different parts of the world. The first wave of migration took place probably about 100000 years ago from Africa to Mediterranean and from there into southern Asia and finally into the Indian sub-continent[9]. It was followed by several waves of migration from Africa, Asia and Europe resulting in the formation of a multiracial and heterogeneous society by

4000 BC. That is characteristic of India even today. Anthropological studies of the prehistoric races based on skeletal studies confirm that many races existed in pre historic India. Sir Herbert Ripley identified seven racial types.

Dr. B. S. Guha [11] identified six main races that migrated to the Indian sub-continent in ancient times. They were the Negritos, the proto Australoid, the Mongoloid, the Mediterranean, the Western Brachycephalic, and the Nordic. There is no evidence to suggest that a new racial type of Caucasian origin had been added to the sub-continent through an Aryan invasion subsequent to the decline of the Indus Valley Civilization.

## Non recognition of the distant past of India:

There has been non recognition of antiquity of India in west due to bias and Eurocentric attitude. Findings of Harappa and other archeological evidence has been totally ignored. It was being said that India had no significant past. The village of Balathal [Udaipur], Rajasthan illustrates antiquity of India's history as it dates back to 4000BC[12].

Balathal was discovered in 1962 and Excavations had not begun till 1990. Archeological excavations in last 50 years have dramatically changed the understanding of India's past. It is now understood that significant human activity existed in India over 10000 years back. Many historical assumptions based on earlier work in Egypt and Mesopotamia needs to be reviewed and revisited. The beginnings of Vedic traditions in India still practiced in India today can now be dated and can be attributed to Balathal than to often claimed to be post Aryan [1500BC]. Around 5500 BC cotton was being cultivated in India.

Analysis of mtDNA dates immigration of Sapiens to India in 75000BC—50000BC[13]. They Spread to Australia in 40000BC. At rock shelters of Bhimbetka humans lived, their cave Paintings date30000BC. Soanian is an archeological culture of lower Paleolithic period [500, 000—125, 000 years] in India[13]. Soanian sites are found along Sivalik region in present day India, Nepal and Pakistan. Neolithic Mehrgarh, Baluchistan lasted from 7000BC—to 5600BC. The ceramic Neolithic period lasted till 3300BC blending with early Harappa Civilization. In South India

Neolithic began 3000BC and lasted till 1400BC. Dravidian Civilization began in 2500BC and Indus civilization began at Harappa in 3500BC.

Indian history has its roots in mythology. Close purview of Puranas, Epics and Rigveda gives us deep insight into India's ancient culture and dynasties who ruled. Submergence of Dwaraka is mentioned in Matysa, Vayu and even in Harivasma. This is not a figment of imagination but a historical reality. Marine archeological explorations have proved existence of submerged Dwarka city. When Rao who was head of these explorations was asked, are you sure it is Dwarka? He replied except for name plate which is not there! In 2001 AD scientists discovered two ancient cities at Gulf of Khambhat. Carbon dating put cities 9500 year old. This means civilization lost at the end of ice age. It also means we could be dealing with a civilization much older than mythical floods. Sangam literature also tells us submergence of east coast 11000 year back when sea level was rising. How long it would have taken civilization that was already there 9500 year ago, to build cities of that scale? This also means 12000 year ago there was a high cultured existence around coasts of India. This was the period when rest of world was sleeping, nowhere near civilization. Why world historians ignoring these finds is any body's guess?

It is Panini who coined "Bharatvarsha" word for this region. Indian subcontinent included present day - "India, Pakistan, Bangladesh, Nepal, Afghanistan and Bhutan". Hindu kush connected India to central Asia and Persia. Archeological explorations and satellite imagery have proved existence of Sarasvati River in ancient India. India is shaped like triangle, with its two coasts on sea, third side in north formed by Himalayas and Hindu Kush mountains. There are writers who believe Kush word is from Lord Rama's son Kush who ruled this area.

Such was then the scenario of prehistoric India which west is bent on to ignore for their Eurocentric history of world.

# INDUS VALLEY CIVILIZATION

Once we talk of civilizations our mind imagines images of Egypt and Mesopotamia [Sumerian].

After 1920 with excavations at Mohanjo Daro and Harappa we have started to think about other Civilizations too. This civilization found around Indus River is being called Indus Valley Civilization. This should be instead called Indo-Saraswat Civilization as this civilization not only flourished around Indus River but around river Saraswati too. Since, this river is not seen today hence conveniently ignored by the writers. Saraswati River has been proved by satellite Photography and its drying up before 1900BC is now well accepted.

Excavations at Harappa and Mohenjo-Daro have established that a thriving urbanized Civilization existed way back in 3300BC. This Civilization was either contemporary to Egypt / Mesopotamia civilizations or preceded it by 100—200 years. People of Mohanjo- Daro and Harappa did not build big monuments nor did they bury their rich in gold tombs. This scenario is quite different from what we see at Egypt and Samaria. This Civilization extended from present day Punjab and Haryana to West Pakistan, involved Rajasthan and parts of present Gujarat. This Size is far bigger than Sumerian civilization. When other civilizations spent lot of their wealth on rich and supernatural, Indus people spent it on common man. These people were very peaceful which is evident from the fact that no weapons of day have been unearthed. More than 1000 sites have been located, excavated and studied which have revealed a lot. An artifact of unique stone Seal carved with a unicorn and inscription has been found. Many other seals with animals and Writings have been unearthed. These writings till date have not been deciphered. Further excavations showed that Harappa society was organized. Buildings were constructed on elevated grounds as area was prone to floods. Buildings were made of bricks and with a definite architectural pattern. There was network of streets and bathing areas. Cleanliness was hallmark of this civilization. Clay figurine of goddesses attests to fact that they practiced and believed in some religion. They domesticated various animals including Cow. Pottery, Textiles and beads Seen give proof of their artisanship. Mode of transport was bull cart. They did built boats as they had maritime trade with Mesopotamia. Trade was of barter system. Mesopotamians called them Meluha. They were called masters of rivers as they built big dams to regulate flow of water to tame floods. They also harvested rain water. Scholars see influence of religion on ritual washing—akin to modern Hindu practices. People got water from wells, had a good sewerage and drainage system in place, and far advanced than seen in contemporary civilizations. One can Judge their architectural skills by looking at their Dockyards, Granaries', Warehouse andProtective walls. Besides cow they domesticated sheep, goat, Bull, Pig. Farmers grew Fruits', Wheat, Peas and some vegetables. Skeletons unearthed showed teeth in good shape, meaning how much they cared for personal hygiene.

Lack of deciphering of their symbols/Seals deprives us of their politics and governance. It was primarily an agricultural society with good network of canals in place. A network of their canal System has been excavated at Lothal. At Dolovaria in Kutch 16 reservoirs have been found.

It is very difficult to know their true religion but continuity with later religions is seen. Swastika, figurine of goddesses, Siva worship seen in them finds continuity till date. They had also achieved mastery in [14]measuring length, mass and time. Various other items found are beads, Painted pottery, 3 headed seal, copper bangles and some golden chain. Lothal, Gujarat served as Port town and manufacturing Centre.

Finding of great bath with stairs leading to bath shows they believed in mass bathing, possibly having some religious association. A seal with person in yogi mudra tells us about their belief in Yogic practices. Dice and toys found tell us type of entertainment they indulged in. There was Outstanding town planning. Indus civilization was primarily a bronze civilization, centered on basin of river Indus and now dried up river Saraswati. This civilization reached its peak between 2600BC-1900BC and then started its fall. What exactly caused its fall is debatable.

Aryan Invasion theorists say that fall occurred as Aryan's with superior military equipment defeated them in battle. There are others who believe climatic catastrophe like floods caused their downfall. Differing versions of this civilization are also there. Article in Encyclopedia Britannica[14] describes Indus civilization Dravidian, came later to Egypt/ Mesopotamia and date it 2500BC—1700BC. It is mentioned that Harappans used Mesopotamian model of irrigation. When Indus civilization antedated Sumerian, how could they borrow their model? There are some who believe that Indus language is partly deciphered. An article from American University[15] dates this", civilization 4500—5000 years old, "Language not deciphered, did not have canal system and down fall due to Aryan invasion". Another article in ancient history dates Indus civilization 5000BC—1500 BC with evidence of religious practices cited. Same article dates Sumerian civilization 5000BC— 1750BC. Indo- Saraswat civilization was much larger than Mesopotamia, more than 1600 sites have been found and are dated between 6500BC— 7000BC by another author[17].

It is quite obvious from above not only we have different dates for this civilization but variance in other details too including its decline. These writers may differ in dates etc.

but one thing is certain that they all now acknowledge its antiquity. [12]

# INDIA AND ARYAN INVASION

A theory of Aryan invasion in 1500BC was invented who came from nowhere and settled in Northern India. They subdue a much advanced society is mind boggling? These so-called Aryans were just nomads breeding cattle for living. British rulers incorporated English language to the detriment of local language in schools. Sanskrit, main language of scriptures was demonized. No educational institution was allowed to teach in Sanskrit. Our culture and traditions were declared superstitions. So much has been brain washing that many a times Indians felt ashamed of themselves. History of India just began with this Aryan invasion [1500BC]?

Several Europeans and a few Indian scholars imagined and argued that speakers of Aryan language must have constituted a single race. Then an attempt was made to find their home land from where they migrated to other places including India. South Russia was suggested their homeland from where they migrated to other places including India. It was Mortimer Wheeler who postulated that destruction of Mohenjo-Daro and Harappa civilization was brought by Invading Aryans from central Asia [Wheeler 1946]? Absence of rice and horse in north India was Cited proof of Aryan invasion. This claim stands now refuted as evidence of rice and horse has been established in Harappa times[18, 19].

Till today we haven't found any evidence of violence between Harapans and so-called Aryan Invaders. There is enough evidence to suggest similarities in religious rites of Harapans and Vedic Aryans. Yoga is also seen practiced in Harappa times, a hallmark of Vedic period. Indus Civilization represents a phase of Indo Aryan civilization when Aryans of India and Iranians lived together in subcontinent and after split Iranians seem to move to Iran.

This scenario started changing after finds of Mohanjo Daro and Harappa in 1922. By now more than 1000 sites have been excavated. It has now been established beyond doubt that India had an advanced civilization around 3500BC, nearly coinciding with Sumerian civilization whose first King was Akaad [2300BC]. West believed that Sumaria was cradle of human civilization but Harappa finds should make west rethink about this issue. Theses Harappan's were having trade

With Mesopotamia. Their language has not been deciphered till date. This civilization ended by 1700BC. In view of new finds there are serious debates now about this so called Aryan invasion to India?

There are different views on this migration of Aryans to India. There are people asserting that no Aryan invasion occurred, asserting Vedic beliefs emerged from Indus valley civilization[13].

Blavatsky believed in Atlantis origin of Aryans who migrated to India and other parts including Europe. There are some who believe in their German origin [Gustaf Kossinna]. This idea was later picked by Nazi's and their claim of Aryan superior race continued till their demise. But there are others who claim Aryans were Indians, Dr Subash kak[20,] Dass[21].

## Those who hold to Aryan invasion:

The proponents of Aryan Invasion hypothesis point to the similarities between Zoroastrianism (the ancient religion of Iran) and the Vedic religion of ancient India. Besides this, similar finds in ancient cemeteries in modern-day India and Tajikistan and Uzbekistan are added factors for invasion. In addition, no trace of horses or chariots in Indus civilization are cited reasons for Aryan invasion.

By 4000 BC, most people in Central Asia, like the Scythians, spoke Indo-European languages. Another migration of these people occurred. Those who went to west became the Hittites, the Greeks, the Romans, and the Germans. Those who went to south-east became the Persians, the Sogdians, and Aryans, who moved into northern India[22, 23].

The Aryans used Chariots and Horses. These were unknown in the sub-continent before their arrival. Aryans conquered the native Dravidian.

They conquered the native Dravidian culture by virtue of their superiority due to their horses & Iron weapons.

The decline of the Indus valley civilization and the abrupt desertion of its settlements could be attributed to Aryan invasion. Vedic Aryans entered India between 1, 500 and 1, 200 B. C according to this theory. Max Muller, the principal architect of the Aryan

Invasion theory, admitted the purely speculative nature of his Vedic chronology, and in his last work published shortly before his death, The Six Systems of Indian Philosophy, he wrote: "Whatever may be the date of the Vedic hymns, whether 15 hundred or 15, 000 B. C., they have their own unique place and stand by themselves in the literature of the world. "

This Aryan Invasion Theory deprives the inhabitants of India of their Vedic heritage when they say, 'The wealth of their culture came from foreign soil.'

Through their political power they, enforced their social and religious life upon the native People. They absorbed the conquered tribes as lower castes in their social order and reserved tribes as Chandalas or the lowest of the lowly.

The Aryan invasion theory has been used for Political and religious advantage in a way that is perhaps unparalleled for any historical idea. [14.] Changing it will thereby alter the very fabric of how we interpret ourselves and our civilization East and West. It is bound to meet with resistance, not merely on rational grounds but to protect the ideologies which have used it to their benefit.

## Those who oppose Aryan invasion:

Since the 1980s, this "Aryan Invasion" hypothesis has been strongly challenged as a myth Propagated by colonial scholars who sought to reinforce the idea that anything valuable in India must have come from elsewhere. Critics of the hypothesis note that there is lack of evidence of any conquest, among other historical and archaeological problems.

The evidence against any such invasion is now far too strong to be taken seriously. To begin With, sites spread over such a vast stretch, measuring well over a thousand miles across would not have been all abandoned simultaneously due to the incursion of nomadic bands at one extremity. Further, there is abundant archaeological evidence including the presence of sacrificial altars that go to show that the Harappans were part of the Vedic Aryan fold. As a result, it can be said that the Vedic age also ended with the Harappan civilization.

Harappan sites contain many sacrificial altars. Such altars suggest a link between Vedic literatures and Harappan archaeology. It also shows that the Vedic literature could not have been brought in by any invaders. Building altars was very much part of the Harappan archaeology! The Sulba- sutra is the oldest mathematical texts known. A careful comparison of the sulba-sutras with the mathematics of Egypt and old Babylonia led Abraham Seidenberg to conclude:

"The elements of ancient geometry found in Egypt and old Babylonia stem from a ritual System of the kind found in the Sulba-sutras."

What is interesting is that the origins of ancient mathematics are to be found in religion and ritual. So, the great engineering feats of the Harappans can be seen as secular off-shoots of the religious mathematics found in Vedic literature. Similarly, the 'ritual mathematics' in the Sulba- sutras led eventually to the purely secular achievements of the Harappans like city planning and the design of harbors.

Frawley's[48] in his very well-documented article demonstrates that there was no Aryan invasion. The author assures us that this theory is widely questioned in the academic world, and that even Scholars who still accept an outside origin for the Vedic people reject the destructive invasion theory to the advantage of migration, diffusion or mixing with indigenous people.

The theory of Aryan invasion has been long debated. While the linguistic evidence suggested a possible relationship between the Vedic people and some inhabitants of ancient Europe, certain Inconsistencies led to its disapproval. Many assumptions have been proved wrong. Based on the new evidence emerging out of the archaeological and anthropological studies, it is now believed that the Vedic tradition was introduced in India much earlier than what Max Muller suggested and that it developed mostly within the sub-continent alongside other traditions.

Frawley shows how recent archaeological findings and a precise reading of Vedic texts invalidate each argument usually accepted to justify the invasion. He also states that the Aryan Invasion theory is an example of

European colonialism turned into an historical model. He very clearly explains how facts and discoveries were molded to fit the "invasion" theory.

**Some arguments put forward against the Aryan invasion are mentioned below:**

1. The native Indians were familiar with horse before the supposed invasion of Aryans.

2. The word Aryan denoted status and position rather than a race or people.

3. There is no evidence of any invasion from outside India until Alexander's time.

4. Vedic religion did not exist outside India. It developed indigenously. Any similarities with neighboring cultural groups may be due to contact rather than common origin.

5. The racial types prevailing in ancient India were the same as those of today.

6. The skeletons found in the excavations do not suggest the arrival of a new racial type.

7. Most of the descriptions of the flora and fauna, the geography and climate mentioned

in Rigveda suggest to their connection with the Indian sub-continent rather than an arctic colder climate.

8. The river systems, constellations mentioned in Rigveda suggest to the existence of the Vedic Culture in India long before the supposed invasion of the Aryans.

9. The excavations at Indus valley urban settlements and the ancient site of Dwarika point to the Continuity of an ancient prehistoric native culture rather than a foreign culture.

10. The battles mentioned in Rigveda such as battle of ten kings were not fought between Aryans and non-Aryans but among different Aryan groups.

11. It is difficult to believe that Sanskrit language of the Rigveda people evolved entirely outside the Indian sub-continent and was brought here by invading Aryan along with their scriptures. There is no evidence of any ancient European tribe or nation ever speaking Sanskrit language.

12. There is no evidence of any European group reciting Vedic mantras or practicing

Vedic rituals based on the hymns contained in the Vedas.

13. India was having a well-developed urban civilization long before the supposed invasion of the Aryans. It is difficult to believe that a group of nomadic and pastoral people would have brought an urban civilization on their horse backs and chariots and introduced it to an already advanced Civilization.

14. There is no evidence of an Aryan homeland outside of India mentioned anywhere in the Vedas.

15. No evidence for a foreign intrusion has been found.

16. There is no archaeological, linguistic, cultural or genetic evidence of invasion.

17. Archaeological finds are culturally consistent, such as the dancing girl, whose bracelets are Similar to those worn by women of Northwest India today.

The three stone Siva Linga found in Harappa by M. S. Vats in 1940. The worship of the Siva Linga is mentioned in the Maha

Narayana Upanishad of the Yajur Veda and is still passionately practiced today.

### *The Vedic Culture is indigenous to India:*

Ancient Vedic literature have an enormous number of Statements and materials presented in it that can be shown to agree with modern scientific findings. They also reveal a highly developed scientific content.

The great Cultural wealth of this knowledge is highly relevant in the modern world. Techniques used to Show this agreement include: Marine Archaeology of underwater sites (such as Dwarika); Satellite imagery of the Indus-Sarasvati River system; Carbon and Thermoluminiscence, dating of archaeological artifacts; Scientific Verification of Scriptural statements; Linguistic analysis of Scripts found on archaeological artifacts etc[24].

### The Sky Epigraphs

Professor Narahari Achar of Memphis University used the pañca. ga Software to locate dates of the celestial events as mentioned by Vyasa in the Mahabharata. This pañca. ga Software was Compiled by a

Japanese professor using the planetarium software called Sky Map by NASA used for calculating the relative movement of the celestial bodies in relation to our earth. He applied it to more than 150 references to the stellar positions that are available In Mahabharata. Prof. Achar mentions of the two Eclipses that happened within the span of fifteen days during the Mahabharata war and the day of the fall of Bhīma and using the pañca. ga software he got the date of the war as having taken place in and around 3000 BCE[30].

Bhabha Atomic Research Centre, tested water from more than 800 bore wells in Rajasthan, on the old Sarasvati River course and did a sophisticated Tritium analysis in the 250-kilometer length of the river bed. It showed that the water of this underground river was of Himalayan glacial Origin and could be dated to be between 8,000 to 14,000 years old[25].

## Vedic Sarasvati River:

Balarama travelled on the banks of river Sarasvati in 3000 BCE, the river Sarasvati was on its final stages of disappearance. Even before Prof. Achar's study, nearly a century ago, one advocate by name Kota Venkatachalam of Tamil Nadu, had come to the same conclusion by a laborious calculation of the celestial events of Mahabharata war using the Ephemeris[26]. Due to geo-physical changes this river shifted its Course. It ran an interrupted course and vanished in to dessert land. Thanks again to archaeological evidence and satellite photography; its full underground terrain has been mapped and is being miraculously restored. The archaeological research work has shown the discovery of Sarasvati River dates back as early as 1812. Lt. Colonel James Todd was the pioneer in this work. In one of his papers, sketch of the Indian desert, he unearthed the evidence of numerous towns and hamlets in the sandy desserts of Rajasthan being scattered and suggested that de-population Occurred in this area due to deficiency of water.

## Sindhu Sarasvati Civilization

While dealing with prehistory and proto-history of the ancient Indian civilization, there is a need to briefly review the story of one of the four oldest world civilizations. The

Sindhu Sarasvati Civilization is unique. It is a unique living vibrant civilization as its thoughts, teachings and traditions are still practiced by vast number of people in the Indian sub-continent grouped under the term 'Hindu's. The land is called as 'Bharatha Varsha'. The story of the Sarasvati River and the Aryan civilization which originated, developed and left a mark on the world is in itself very charming. The Sarasvati River itself was a life line of Aryan civilization and features notably in Rigveda. This civilization was dependent on the abundant flow of Sarasvati River which had its Source in the Himalayas. The Sarasvati River nourished vast territories of land that the river itself and its name were sacred as a Goddess. True to the spirit of Aryan civilization, the river goddess was not named for her bounty and material riches that she provided; but for knowledge and enlightenment of the people who depended upon her. It was a vast river along with its tributaries. Its flow and volume was gigantic – it's width at points exceeding ten to twelve kilometers. Sarasvati, is a river of past. It no longer flows as a regular river. The Indian subcontinent was the Scene of dramatic upheavals a few thousand years ago. The Northwest region entered a dry Phase, and erosion coupled with tectonic events played havoc with river courses. One of them disappeared. Celebrated as Sarasvati in the Rig Veda and the Mahabharata, this river was rediscovered in the early nineteenth century through topographic explorations by British Officials. Of late, geological studies have probed its evolution and disappearance, while satellite imagery has traced the river's buried courses. The isotope analyses have dated ancient waters still Stored under the Thar Desert. In the same Northwest, the subcontinent's first urban society, the Indus civilization flourished and declined. But it was not watered by the Indus alone. Since Aurel Stein' s expedition in the 1940s, hundreds of Harappans sites have been identified in the now dry Sarasvati basin. The rich Harappans legacy in technologies, arts and culture sowed the seeds of Indian civilization as we know it now, [18]. Sarasvati indeed lives in her proven riverbed, confirmed by many archaeological explorations and vividly pictured by satellite photography. Many scientists of the world, both from India and other countries – prominent among them from France, UK, Europe, and Germany have contributed to the growing knowledge about this river. And in a sense have resurrected the 'Mythical long lost dormant river' of Vedic age, providing evidence not only to the time and life of Rig-Vedic age, but to mythology itself.

Historically India has been known as Aryavarta, land of Aryans. Ancestors of Aryans may have come from Africa or elsewhere but Aryan culture is indigenous and derived from Kshatriya clans of Vedic civilization. By usage and customs there is clear evidence that India had a deep and historic connection with concept of Arya. Nowhere is there historical evidence in central Asia/ Russia where by one could say that Aryans lived there and then migrated to India. Aryan invasion theory was mooted by western writers [Max Muller and others] to show superiority of West over East. Even their date of migration [1500BC] is faulty. Their theory that theses Aryans [Nomads] defeated advanced Indus people and in a span of just 100 years formed a mighty Civilization [Vedic civilization] and they fought Mahabharata war in 1400BC --- is **unbelievable**. Civilizations take centuries to make. Again we see this 1500BC date is misleading as it excludes many historical events prior to 1500BC, namely rule of Solar and Lunar dynasties in India.

**Ishvaku** founder of solar dynasty is supposed to have ruled around 8000BC. Its last ruler was Sumitra who was defeated by Nanda In 400BC[27]. Nanda was later ousted by legendary Chandragupta Maurya. **Lunar** dynasty whose first ruler was Yayti is believed to have ruled— 3500BC[44]. There were 47 rulers between Yayti and Yudhishthira, Hero of Mahabharata war. Why are these facts being ignored by western writers? Just sticking to 1500 BC invasion theory means negating India's past and its glory. There are historical data suggesting that **Brihadratha** dynasty ruled India much before 1700BC, **Pradyota** dynasty 799BC[28] and **Haryanka** dynasty in 684BC. How could these dates fit in to Aryan invasion [1500BC]? Hastinapur and Kosala dynasties are supposed to have ruled from 3067BC— 1563BC, Brihadratha dynasty ruled around 3067BC followed by Pradyota, Haryanka, Shisunga dynasties.

How could Rigveda, earliest manuscript of mankind be written[30] in 250—300BC? Lord Buddha [563BC—483BC] denounced various Brahmanical rituals mentioned in Rigveda. It means Rigveda must have been written quite earlier. Saraswati River is mentioned in Rigveda 50 times.

Satellite imagery has established that Saraswati River dried up before 1900BC which means Rigveda must have been written quite earlier [3000BC] as mentioned by some. Dwarka, city of Lord Krishna has been located by marine archeologist [Rao]. It is now established that Dwarka got submerged in sea in 1500BC---1600BC. [19]

## A pertinent question for invasion theorists:

Why would invaders praise Saraswati River in their literature which had dried up long back? [3000BC]. This means absurdity of Aryan invasion in 1500BC.

Indian ancient history needs to be rewritten. Indus seals when deciphered showed prakrit/ Sanskrit as its Language, whole thesis of Aryan invasion went down in history as greatest bluff spread by West. There are writers who believe Indus civilization is post Vedic. Prof Winternitz[31] thinks that beginning of Vedic literature goes back to 2000BC---2500BC. Prof MacDonnell[32] says Importance of Indian literature lies in its originality. Pilny and Arrian, Greek historians have even identified 154 kings between Lord Rama and Chandragupta [321BC]. Sanderson Beck in his book, "Literature of India" says that Ramayana and Mahabharata could have occurred around 12000BC---10000BC[33]. B. G. Tilak, [The Orion, into antiquity of Vedas, Bombay 1893], dates Vedic civilization between 4000---8000 years. Historian BB Lal gives 5700BC—1400BC as time period of Lord Krishna [19]. Prof Achar of Memphis University after studying planetary positions mentioned in Srimad Bhagwat has dated Mahabharata war 3067BC. [34]

Some other dates suggested are:

Manu Vivastava 3102BC.
Lord Rama 5114BC-1950BC.
Dasaraja war 1900BC.
Mahabharata war 3138BC.

In Valmiki Ramayana for some important events planetary positions have been amply described. Taking advantage of this P.

Bhatnagar[80] has come out with 5114 BC as date of birth of Lord Rama, 5089BC as date of coronation and killing of Megnath 24th Nov 5076BC. Ramsetu, bridge Connecting India with Lanka is one of the relics of Ramayana time present even today, confirmed by satellite photography. This bridge was being used as foot bridge as late as 1480AD when it got submerged in water. Even Al- Baruni [1030AD] mentions about this bridge in his book. Isn't it enough proof to say that Aryan invasion theory is a lie? How can we ignore ancient historical India just to please pseudo and prejudiced western scholars who want to snub India's Wisdom and its glorious past? Instead of declaring Ram Setu as national heritage, some unscrupulous elements are bent on to dismantle it for navigation purposes. What a shame? Possibly wanting a western certification for Ram Setu existence?

There have been deliberate attempts to misinterpret Vedas. Karl Sagan acknowledges that Cosmology of Vedas is akin to science. Oppenheimer, Emerson, German philosopher Shophauner also acknowledge authenticity of Vedas. It is interesting to note that we have 2500 archeological sites without corresponding literature. At the same time we have abundant Vedic literature without much archeological evidence. Could it be both civilizations were Complimentary to each other or were running parallel? Vedic culture looks to be indigenous through archeology, cultural continuity and by linguistic analysis. Language and symbolism in Indus seals [swastika, banyan tree, OM, Shiv Puja] are Vedic in origin. Vedas are real and not Mythical as originally thought.

Sahoo, Kivisild, Metspalu etel in 2006[35, 36] stated that concept of people, Language, Agriculture arriving in India through northwest corridor does not hold to scrutiny. Metspalu in 2004 further stated that it is mt DNA lineage of M and N which originated in India which has populated whole Europe and west Asia and not vice versa. This is genetic proof of Aryan Indian origin.

We should here clarify what word Arya means? Word means just noble, it has nothing to do with race or language. Arya denotes certain spiritual and humanistic values and whole Vedic Civilization was driven and sustained by these values. So, anyone who lived by these set rules was called Arya. This was irrespective of race and language. It also means people living in India be it from north or south [Dravidian] could be called Aryan if upholding Vedic values. Aryan Invasion was intellectual creation of west who wanted to get rid of Jewish heritage of Christianity. One reason of this invasion theory could be biblical belief that whole human race descended from son of Noah who survived flood [2500BC] and Adam and Eve were borne just in 4004BC. Great deal of British Indology was motivated by Christian missionary considerations.

Max Muller was a Christian missionary. This racial theory was replaced by Linguistic invasion When Max Muller faced opposition. He changed his stance to language based invasion for selfish Interests. There has never been any scientific basis for Aryan invasion. This was used as a tool of Propaganda and to denigrate any good of East. If we give some thought to this invasion theory, it means Sanskrit and Vedas had foreign origins. Then question comes, is there a country where Sanskrit is spoken and Vedas are its literature outside India? Answer is blunt **NO**. India is only Country in world where Sanskrit is known, spoken and its literature and culture is Veda based. Horse was known to Indians long before 1500BC. Dereivka horse unearthed in Ukraine, dated 4000BC later proved to be hoax. Plenty of horse fossils have been now found in Punjab. This clearly shuts argument that horse came from outside in to India. Seven rivers [sapt Sindhu], constellations mentioned in Rigveda refer to India and not any other country.

Doesn't above debunk linguistic Invasion and race invasion of India?

Linguistic paleontology has been used to construct Aryan and Proto indo European culture. John Muir [quoted by Das] stated, "Various Indo-European people have sprung from the gradual dispersion of the ancient Aryan race of India. " Indeed all Europeans, many Africans can have their ancestry to only 4mtDNA which appeared between 10, 000—50, 000 years ago and Originated in India. Aryan invasion model based largely on linguistic conjectures is totally unjustified[21.] It is saddening to see that modern Indian scholars are not coming up with realistic version of history. They continue on worn out paths and rely on western translations of

Vedic literature which is biased and Eurocentric. Many of the Indian scholars have a handicap of not knowing Sanskrit so fall on western opinion. Indian historians should have really pondered on this idea, "Why Germans are looking to land and culture far away from their land"? This is a scholarship failure. Eurocentric domination of Indian intellectuals. It is a very sad story. We still are slaves to West even after independence. We seem to have developed inferiority complex after foreign rule of over 500 years. Indian scholars should wake, read original Sanskrit books instead of western translations. Then only can they rewrite India's past history with all honesty. Let me add some quote here:

-Hegel, philosopher said, "Germans were pupils of Indian sages. "

# VEDIC ARYANS

There is not one word in our scriptures, not one, to prove that the Aryans ever came from anywhere from outside India. Swami Vivekananda said, "The whole of India is Aryan, nothing else". He further stated clearly: "Such words as Aryans and Dravidians are only of philological import, the so called Craniological differentiation finding no solid ground to work upon." Any theory worth its salt Should provide clarity of vision. But not so, the Aryan race concepts. Swami Vivekananda correctly pointed out that they instead provide only "a lot of haze, created by a too adventurous Western philology". Today the tools of science have changed. Today it is not "craniological differentiation" but nucleotide markers in Y-chromosomes, and what Swami Vivekananda Stated remains true today. The nucleotide markers emphatically reject any invasion from outside India.

Archaeologists again and again state that they fail to trace any movement or invasion into India. Archaeologists even speak of cultural continuities for more than five thousand years with no invasion based break in that continuity… Swami Vivekananda[37].

Greatest bluff of modern times is that Aryans came from outside, defeated locals and settled in India in 1500BC. This means to negate all historical events of India before 1500BC. This is completely unsound. Vedas were given by people of India who had been living in India for thousands of years. Archeologists at Harvard, Oxford now agree that there was no Aryan Invasion that displaced Indus people. Vedic culture was either precursor to Indus civilization or early contributor to its culture. This is documented by Professor K. Chandler in his book, "Origin of Vedic civilization" [38].

Vedic civilization arose in India long before various suggested dates. Linguistic similarities between European, Iranian and Indian languages made some authors to suggest common origin. This made Sir William Jones to suggest in 1786 that these languages have common source which no longer exists. Schlegel of Germany went as far as to say that European languages are derived from Sanskrit[39]. This infuriated western scholars because Sanskrit as mother of European languages hurt their Eurocentric ideology. To circumvent this they devised a theory that people speaking proto-indo-European came from west Asia/ SE, Europe, invaded India and settled there. It is from India they came to Iran. These Indo-Europeans were later called Aryans. In twentieth century Germans Conceived them as Germans, an idea later taken up by Nazi's[23.]

In 1990's with new scientific evidence coming from satellite photography, geological study and Archeological excavations have discredited this invasion theory. Professor Renfrew[40] of Cambridge gives evidence of Indo-Europeans in India as early as 6000BC. Professor Schaffer[41]Writes, development of civilization in India goes back 6000BC. He further adds that Rigveda Which initially was Saraswati based, later became Ganges based literature due to drying up of river Saraswati [1900BC]. He proposed Indus civilization between 2600BC-1900BC.

By postulating invasion theory authors ignored India's traditional history and even Vedic literature.

Other civilizations have left their mark by way of written documents and inscriptions. In India Writing came very late. Till writing came everything was transmitted orally. Purana writings were declared myth by west as its write up did not match up to western impressions about India. It is true Puranas deal with creation of Universe, gods, demons but they do write about history. Later Writers not only have interpolated them but put in additional material in them, which makes it difficult for a subsequent reader to separate historical event from added material. This makes some to doubt their authenticity. Nowhere in Puranas and in Rigveda are we told about foreign Land/home?

How did this invasion theory originate? Europeans who were trading with India had to find alternative route as land route through Arab world got jammed because of conflict between Christians and Muslims. West found sea route and in order to show their superiority they had to devise various means to prove it. One of the means they invented was Invasion theory. Secondly, they demonized local traditions and beliefs. Local language Sanskrit was ignored and English

Was forced on common man. It was postulated that India was no man's land, people came from Outside and gave it a civilization. Now question for them was to find which country they came from? This home land had different connotations for different people. Nordic, Iranian, Atlantis, German and South Russia [Central Asia] were countries mooted as home land of so called Aryan People, who invaded India and date fixed was 1500BC. Out of these homeland countries CentralAsia [South Russia] has maximum votaries. Linguistic paleontology has been used as a tool to Construct Aryan culture and proto Indo-European culture. There is really no proof to prove what Language South Russian [Kurgs] spoke at the time of this so called migration. Totally hypothetical, only Eurocentric scholars stick to this hypothesis. It was suggested that horse was Unknown to Indian's and these Aryans came on horses to India and defeated locals to establish themselves. But it may be mentioned here that horse was known animal in Punjab, India as far back as 2500BC. Plenty of horse fossils have been found in India giving lie to people who said Horse came from outside to India[42]. Dereivka horse, unearthed in Ukraine dated

4000BC proved later to be hoax. Close association of Indo-Europeans with horse does not[24]show any connection With Russia but with India. Similarities between Indo-Europeans and Austronesian cultures Indicate India was the original homeland. DNA studies have shown Cows moved from India to Ukraine and not vice versa. Sun, Fire and animal worship are seen in all ancient civilizations. Just to deduce inferences from these practices is highly erroneous.

Road map given by invasion theorists: --- Indo-European to Central Asia, then two branches, one goes to Iran and other comes to India. We will show later that it is from India people went to Iran and Europe and not vice versa.

Word **Aryan** applies to language and not race, said Max Muller, a profounder of invasion theory. But later writers conveniently used Aryan for race. This means invasion theorists who based their theory on linguistic premise where replaced by race invasion.

T. Burrow[43] admits Aryan invasion of India is not recorded in any document, nor can be traced archeologically. John Muir quoted by Das states, "that various Indo-European people have sprung from the gradual dispersion of the ancient Aryan race of India, such dispersion being occasioned by political/religious causes". Iranian tradition tells us that their ancestors came from **Outside** but nowhere Rigveda tells Vedic people entered Punjab from outside. It is clear that Dravidians was spoken in south India and Indo-European in north India and not in South Russia as claimed by Invasionists.

Archeologist Mark Kenoyer[45] holds that invasion theory is completely unsupported by linguistic, literary and Archeological evidence. Kenoyer holds that Indus script can be traced at least 3300BC. Archeologist Kennedy[46] states no Aryan skeletons have been Found in Indus valley different from skeletons of indigenous ethnic groups.

**Rigveda** nowhere mentions about migration or some homeland outside India. All evidence be it Archeological, Anthropological and Vedic literature point to Vedic civilization was indigenous to Northwest India. Geological data also suggests demise of Indus civilization to climatic change than to invasion.

When Vedic people did not come from outside, how could their language come from outside? It is logical to think that their language which was Sanskrit came from the place of their living and that is India. Sanskrit went with them to Iran and Europe where they went later. Vedic Civilization came around 1000BC—1200BC is putting cart before horse. These dates are west created to suite their Eurocentric ideology. It is interesting to note that Max Muller who Postulated invasion theory was a believer of biblical date of creation, which is 4004 BC. He had to fit in dates accommodating biblical ideas of world. Same author in his later writing wrote, "Vedas are great wisdom whatever be their date 1500BC or 15000BC". Different western authors have given different dates of this civilization depending on their personal dispensation and ignoring scientific evidence. Encyclopedia Britannica dates early Vedic civilization to[14] 1500BC—800 BC and late Vedic civilization to 800BC—500 BC. These dates easily ignore various ancient historical events. **Rigveda**, oldest human scripture mentions Saraswati

River 60 times in its narrative. And this river dried up earlier than 1900BC. River Saraswati was reduced to trickle by 3000BC and dried up completely by 1900BC. From this one can easily surmise that that Rigveda must have been written much earlier than 3000BC as in Rigveda Saraswati River is described as mighty river. Rajaram[47] puts beginning of Vedic tradition, no later than 3500BC and its end before 2000BC. Mahabharata describes Saraswati River as a seasonal river. Since it dried up completely by 1900BC, Mahabharata should be before 1900 BC. Since it still is a seasonal river, Rajaram and Frawley[48] put date of Mahabharata in 3000BC. If Rigveda tradition began before 3500BC, this would **antedate** it to Harappa and Mesopotamia.

Maurice Winternitz[49] German writer put Vedic tradition at some time before2400BC, bare minimum. If Mahabharata occurred around 3000BC and we add 1900 years as incubation time as Suggested by Winternitz for civilization to evolve then date of Rigveda jumps to 4900 BC. By using astronomical data Tilak[50] dated Rigveda 6000BC.

Some of the dates given by Frawley[51] are:

6500BC-3100BC. This he called **Pre-Harappans**, early Vedic. [Period 1]

3100BC-1900BC. This he called **mature Harappa**, period of 4 Vedas. [Period 2]

1900BC-1000BC. This he labeled **late Harappa**, late Vedic and Brahmana period. [Period 3]

Professor Aggarwal gives following dates:

**Rigveda**--------------------7000BC-4000BC.

**End of vedic** age ----------------------3750BC.

**End of Ramayana** and Mahabharata period-------------------------------------------3000BC.

**Development** of Indus civilization--------------------------------------------3000BC-2200BC.

Dr Siddarth dates Rigveda ----------------1000BC.

Such is variance in dates that these have become subject of big discussion now.

Kenoyer[53] anthropologist shows one seal of Indus valley civilization showing deity in yoga position. This further shows Indus civilization was not prevedic. If Indus people practiced yoga, adopted sthapatya Vedic architecture for building, it means Vedic traditions were well established in India during Indus valley civilization. A stone has been unearthed in Western India having Devanagari script. It is dated 3000BC.

Vedic tradition was oral to start with, script came much later. Winternitz puts Vedic traditions before 4900BC according to his formula[54].

Text books still talk of Mesopotamia as cradle of human civilization ignoring finds of **Mehrgarh** [6500BC---7000BC], Vedic civilization and even Harappa civilization. How long back urban Civilization began in India is difficult to know. Archeology has shown that people who were hunter gatherers lived in India 40000 years back. 100, 000 years back there were humans in India Who had 20th century man's brain size. Stone axes, other primitive chopping tools have been found in northern India dating to 500, 000 BC[55]. Since Vedic traditions started orally, writing came late, and it is difficult to date them exactly but for sure before

3000BC, putting nail on invasion theory [1500BC]. There is evidence of Continuity of same people with same traditions from ancient till present. Mahabharata lists whole Course of river Saraswati hence has to be before drying up river Saraswati, 3000BC. Vedic Society is much more open, Creative and Spiritual. Caste system came much later due to greed of Brahmins who wanted to dominate society.

5000BC Paintings have been found in Brahm Kund Ki Dungari and Budhi Jeengore in Rajasthan.

This Vedic civilization is much older than Egypt and Mesopotamia. Times of India, dated 30.5.1992, published an article showing prehistoric paintings on Kanera rocks, Rajasthan dating 50,000—60,000 year old. Science magazine, 23. 2. 2010, reported how people lived before and after Colossal Toba volcanic eruption 74000 years ago in India. This shows presence of **man** in India Long before other civilizations on earth. Linguists date, Rigveda 1000BC which is highly erroneous. Rigveda mentions river Saraswati in Its text. When we know with reasonable certainty that river Saraswati dried before 1900BC, how can we accept linguist date as correct one? For Tilak Vedic period began in 4500BC[57] and bulk of hymns of Rigveda were composed between 3500BC-2500BC. Astronomical observations in Rigveda and in other texts including Puranas are best and reliable evidence in dating these texts. Dharampal[58] states in his write up that Indian zodiac originated in 4300BC and rejects any idea of astronomical statements in Sanskrit texts being fabrications. Why would Aryans who came to India in 1500BC [invasion theorists] talk about river Saraswati in their text when same river had dried up long back [3000BC]? This should be food for thought for invasion theorists.

**Rigveda** is not a history book but a book speaking about human mind. It does provide geographical data by mentioning various places and its narrative also writes about Kings.

Rigveda hymns clearly show Indo-European language speaking people of time lived in Punjab, Bihar and in Rajasthan, Afghanistan and up to Maharashtra. Its various recensions have not come down to us in complete form.

It is absurd to suppose that elaborate royal genealogy shown in texts is a figment of imagination of writers. Puranas give traditional history. Scene opens with division of territories among sons of Manu. Traditional account does not speak of Aryan Invasion nor does it say about any conflict between Aryans and non-Aryans.

Just as four **Vedas** described human mind in hymns, Puranas besides other things give general list of various dynasties along with traditions down to the time of Mahabharata. There are 18 Puranas. Brahma Purana, Vayu purana and Matsya are oldest. So we should be looking for history in Puranas than in Vedas. It is absurd to think that royal genealogy presented in them is Imaginary. it is important while giving opinion on matter. We should take opinion of both Vedas and Puranas together. Puranas commence with traditional history, 10 sons of Manu, **Ishavaku**, founder of solar dynasty is one of them[27]. Lord Rama belonged to solar dynasty. From Sudyumna kingdom we get Puru and Yadu dynasty. It is from Yadu dynasty we get Lord Krishna. Other dynasties are not mentioned here as their role in future history of India is limited. . Puranas, Epics, and local traditions locate Ishavaku dynasty to Ayodhya. It is king Bhagirathi of this dynasty who founded Kosala kingdom. Combined evidence of Vedas and Puranas cannot be faulted and accused of conspiracy. Vedas and Puranas are being accused of conflicting versions of history. The fact Vedas seem to confirm the Puranic accounts is a proof of validity as geography mentioned is matching in both. Kings found in Vedas are found in traditional Puranas also. Many events antedate Rigveda hence logical to conclude that puranas should have talked about outside homeland. This also **invalidates** invasion theory.

Puranas locate different dynasties in different parts of northern India. Purus are located in Punjab. Ved Samhita gives us evidence of movement of Aryans from Punjab to other parts of north—east. According to puranas ancestors of Puru, Anus and DRUHYUS lived in south east Uttar Pradesh. Same purana tells us later they migrated west wards and divided themselves into various groups. Purus occupied Punjab, Anus went to Kashmir and nearby areas and DRUHYUS went into North West Punjab [present Afghanistan]. Puranas provide incontrovertible evidence that ultimate homeland of Indo-Europeans lay in northern India [homeland of Vedic Aryans and Iranians]. Rigveda is good source to tell us and corroborates historical events mentioned in Puranas.

Iranian and west Asian mythologies have direct links with Vedic mythology. Even East European mythology has some common elements with Vedic mythology. Vedic culture and language stands senior to Iranian, West Asian and European languages and culture. Rigveda and Puranas provide strong evidence that India was homeland to Indo-European family of languages. Later Vedic culture spread all over India. ANUS spread to West Asia and Druhyus to Europe. This is real picture of Aryans and their spread to West Asia and Europe. Road map given by invasionists that Aryans came from central Asia is proved false and fraudulent.

How long back urban civilization begin in India? Archeology has shown us that hunter gatherers lived in central India 40, 000BC. As early as 100, 000 years there were humans in India with 20th century man's brain size. Stone axes other primitive tools over 4-5 thousand old have been found in northern India. Since Vedic tradition started orally, it has left no foot prints in stones, difficult to date. But certainly, it dates before 3000BC, possibly even earlier. What is certain is that Max Muller date of 1500BC invasion is a **blunt Lie.**

. **Science and math** originated in India and went to Greece much later. Zend Avesta of Persia took many names from Vedic pantheon. Mitra, Indra, Varuna are seen in seals of treaty between Hittites and Mitanni. This shows Vedic influence in Mediterranean before Trojan War. Many Greek gods are similar to Vedic gods. This shows influence of Vedic civilization on Greece. This cannot be other way round as Vedic civilization preceded Greek civilization. India remained light house for advance of any civilization on earth.

We will end this chapter with quote of Mark Twain" India is cradle of the human race, birth place of human speech, the mother of history, the grandmother of legend and great grandmother of tradition. Our most valuable and most constructive materials in history of man are treasured up in **INDIA** only".

# GENETICS AND ARYAN ORIGIN

We have seen till now that there is no written document [Vedic texts included] and Archeological evidence to prove that Aryans came from outside, defeated locals and founded a Civilization here. On the contrary we have proved in this write up that Aryans were Indians and they spread out from India to Iran and Europe.

Now let us see what gene migration tells us about origins of Aryans. Presently we see DNA tests are done to prove or disapprove a legal claim, prove parentage, trace culprits and so on. This is due to fact that DNA testing is trustworthy and highly reliable. Finding of oldest human mtDNA in Africa became basis for African **EVE** and human origin.

Modern human subspecies spread from Africa, road map given of this migration bypassed India. It may be mentioned here LO, L1, L2, L3, mtDNA has been found in some tribes of Africa. From Africa we are told that L3 gene moved out and road map given to us tells that this African Gene went to Europe and from there to Central Asia to India. It has now been found that rest of the world had been populated from mtDNA lineage of M and N and Place of origin of both were found to be India.

In India DNA testing has shown that Indians have M and N type genes. These are supposed to be daughters of L3 which migrated from Africa. It is interesting to note that we don't have M and N outside India. M and N are basic lineages of these areas, their oldest portions still found in India.

Then N split into R and U. M and N branched and spread further after originating from India. R Which is branch of N is seen in China and Southeast Asia. U is another branch of N which is found in Europe. Kivisild[59] proved that U originated in India. First migration from India went to Australia and Southeast Asia. Metspalu who studied over 50, 000 genes came to conclusion that Asia, Europe and America have genes which originated in India. He further said that IndianDNA is oldest one. His paper is quoted by Dr Priyadharshi[60]. U is predominant in Europe, WestAsia and India. Presence of U in Europe and in India made 'Invasion' theorists to claim that Aryans coming to India from west. They completely forgot what

Kivisild had said, "U originated from N, home land of N is India". U5a is a derivative of U which originated from N [is found in Europe]. Narmada man, a human fossil found in Hathnora, Gujarat, India is being dated 250, 000 years old. Kennedy[61], an anthropologist believes that this is oldest Homo sapiens Unearthed with cranial capacity of 1500ml which is close to modern man dimension. DaLumle and Sonakia again quoted by Priyadharshi state that Narmada man could be ancestor to all Indians. Malasse Dabricourt says African skull lacks Taurus angularis hence cannot be our Ancestor. But Taurus angularis is seen in Rhodesia man who came from India[62]. DNA studies have demolished myth that India was" No man's land'. It is from India that rest of the world got populated. This is further corroborated by Kumar whose study shows that 15000 years back people migrated out of India to South Asia.

Kivisild[63] wrote genetic heritage of earliest settlers within Indian tribal and caste system is still Persisting. This disapproves the theory that man stayed in India for short time, went out and Came back to India. Genetically in

India we see no north or south as there has been enough Hybridization amongst two.

Sahoo etal[64.] The perennial concept of people, language and Agriculture arriving in India together through northwest corridor does not hold up to scrutiny. Recent claims for a linkage of haplo group J2, L R1a and R2 with a contemporaneous origin for the majority of the Indian castes, paternal lineages from the outside the subcontinent are rejected, although our findings do Support a local origin of haplogroup F and H".

Ukraine received Cows from India has been shown by Kantanen in his study[65]. Underhill 2009 [66] states absence of M45 8 chromosome outside Europe speaks against substantial patrilineal gene from East Europe to Asia and India. Oppenheimer [70] rejects 3500 BP arrival of Caucasians in India.

He further states, "Just as imaginary invasion theory has left no written records or archeological Imprints, it is invisible at genetic level too". M17 as a marker for Aryan invasion is rejected. It is suggested M17 could have come to Europe via Central Asia after reaching there from India.

Indeed, all European and some Africans can trace their ancestors to South Asia[67]. A genetic Connection between India and Europe has been established though very old [50, 000 years]. Indian MtDNA has been seen not subdividing according to linguistic or caste lines. Subcontinent's gene Landscape was formed long before proposed Aryan invasion. There is also evidence that Dravidian pool has Indian origin. In fact, Luis Quintana-Murci[68], Macaulay[69], Oppenheimer [70] have proposed that H. Sapiens migrated out of Africa, reached South West Asia around 75000 BP and then moved to other parts of world. It means except for Africans; all humans have Ancestors in North West of Indian peninsula. Indeed, nearly all Europeans and many Americans can trace their ancestry to South Asia [Allman WF][71].

Oppenheimer[70] wrote, "For me and Kivisild South Asia is logically the ultimate origin of M17 and his ancestors. We find high diversity of M17 in Pakistan, India, and East Iran than in Caucasus. M17 is not only more diverse in South Asia than in Central Asia but diversity Characterizes its presence in isolated tribes of South thus undermining theory of M17 as marker of invasion of

Aryans. M17 could have gone from India through Kashmir to Central Asia, Russia and finally to Europe". It may be mentioned here that Aryan invasion theorists were Postulating M17 as a marker for their imaginary theory. This marker stands debunked by above. Even Michel Danino traces genetics and Aryan debate on same lines [73].

In view of above road map of gene migration is as follows: --- From Africa L3 gene moves to India. Genes M and N develop in India. M and N migrate out of India and spread. N in due course mutates in to R [seen in China, South Asia] and U which is seen in Europe. U further mutates in to U5a seen in Europe.

**In conclusion** genetics also debunks colonial history of telling world that Aryans invaded India in 1500BC. This Eurocentric and biased attitude of western scholars needs to be changed. India needs to be given due place in history and its role in providing world a top-class civilization, where motto of life was to know unknown, needs to be acknowledged.

**Will Durant**, "India was the mother land of our race and Sanskrit the mother of Europe's languages. India was the mother of our philosophy, much of our mathematics, of the ideals embodied in Christianity............ In many ways, mother India is the mother of all of us". Mind You Durant was American historian, not Indian.

# VEDIC ARYANS AND THEIR CIVILIZATION

It is a period during which Vedas and other texts were composed/written. This period according to western writers started after Aryans came from somewhere in central Asia in 1500BC, dates already refuted by us. We have shown earlier that Aryans did not come from outside but were Indian residents. When they did not come from outside so language, they have is totally Indian, which is Sanskrit. There is a strong possibility that Sanskrit is mother of Proto-Indo-European Languages. Often talked Aryan and Dravidian conflict is a myth [TOI Sept25, 2009]. There is tremendous confusion about word "Aryan". Max Muller, proponent of invasion believed word applied to language. But there are writers to whom word means Race. Puranas and Epics do talk of migration outside to establish kingdoms but not Aryans coming from outside. Vishnu purana11. 3. 1, written nearly 2000 years back writes" Bharata" is a country north of ocean and South of snowy mountains. This clearly explodes myth that Britishers made country, India as it exists today. Epics written have been rewritten and modified depending on local traditions.

Heroes are deified and their achievement's exaggerated to immortalize them. But attempt always has been to stick to basic story. This gives them authenticity of history. A dense network of "Tirths" and other holy sites has led to creating sacred geography of India. This has helped in national integration plus preserved rich culture till today. There is no mention of Aryans as white and non-Aryans as black in old texts available. Initially everything was transmitted orally.

Writing came late hence some doubt their genuineness. One needs to read Vedic texts along Puranas to come to firm conclusion. Reading them separately can lead to erroneous conclusions.

Puranas locate different dynasties in different parts of India.

Coming to Aryans it is clear they were tribals, pastoral society. These people were in search of fresh pastures which they found in Gangetic belt. These people took along with them whatever they could take with them including local traditions. Aryans lived in tribes and with passage of time each tribe established its own area and later kingdom. King became absolute ruler and Brahmin enjoyed high place in society. Agriculture was there main profession. Western scholars who believe they came from outside believe that they brought with them distinctive religiousPractices and traditions, a belief which can be contested. Rigveda describes a conflict between Bharatas whose chief was Sudas against a confederation of ten kings. This battle was fought near river Ravi. Ten tribes which joined hands against Bharata's were Puru, Yadu, Turvasha, Anu, Druhyu, Alina, Bhalanas, Pktha, Siva and Vishanm. This battle was won by Sudas. "Here the remarkable tradition recorded that Paijavana, i. e. , Sudas who was so famous for his sacrifices and who is celebrated in the Rig Veda as the patron of Vishwamitra and enemy of Vashishta, was a Shudra. "Sudas was a king and his coronation ceremony was performed by the Brahma-Rishi, Vashishta. Later Bharata's and Purus merged in to one and formed Kuru dynasty.

This Kuru kingdom was also joined by other tribes. Vedic religion started shaping up later. Vedic hymns were collected and transcribed and new rituals developed. Vedic religion amalgamated some native culture in it. Later caste system developed. Aryan society was Egalitarian. Vedic house hold was patriarchal and patrilineal. Institution of marriage was Important and sacrosanct too. People consumed milk products, vegetable and fruits. Meat also was consumed; its prohibition came much later when various philosophies took shape. There was division of labour which later turned in to caste system. Emergence of monarchial states later led to emergence of Varaha hierarchy. Economy was pastoralism and agriculture. Early Vedic age was a bronze age. And the late Vedic period was Iron Age. They had various professions such as Warriors, Priests, Framer, Artisan and Craftsman to name a few. Vedic forms of belief are one of the precursors of modern Hinduism. People believed in transmigration of Souls, after life. Many of the concepts of Indian philosophy adopted later like Dharma, Karma etc. trace their roots to Vedas. Ritualistic traditions of Vedic religion are preserved in traditional Srauta tradition. Srauta tradition lays emphasis on ritual. Horse sacrifice [Ashvamedha] started being practiced. A horse will be let loose, if horse is caught by someone/king then a battle with the Person/king will be fought. The Looser had to give booty to winner. Soma and Sura were popular drinks. People used Cotton, Wool, and Animal skin for clothing. Brahmin was symbol of purity, good conduct and teaching. Kshatriya associated with strength, fame and rule. Vaishya involved in business and Shudras were involved in service of higher Varnas. Household was an important Unit headed by Grihapti.

This Vedic period is traditionally described in two periods, Early and Late. **Early period** is from 1750 BC--- 1000BC and **Late period** is from 1000BC---500BC. This traditional dating also shows Aryan invasion [1500BC is fictitious]. In early period Rigveda starts religious hymns and various stories and myths. There is mention of political organization, Social and Economic order. Varnas, Agriculture and details of types of marriage etc. are written. Vedic religious practices are written in detail. Main deities mentioned are Indra, Agni, Soma, and Mitra-Varuna, Sun, Vayu, Prithivi, Aditi [mother of gods. ] Universe origin, yoga and some elements of Vedanta philosophy are mentioned.

**Late Vedic period** [1000BC—500BC]: Concept of marriage and its rules become strict so gets Varna order. Various Kingdoms are mentioned in detail including their jurisdiction.

Mahajanapadas take birth. Kshatriyas become powerful and service of Brahmins is utilized in governance. King became all powerful. Agriculture is mentioned as main economy hence attempt to grab land which would mean war also with neighbor. The compilation of Mahabharata and Ramayana was done in this period. In the late Vedic period, Samhitas, Brahmana prose and Sutra language takes birth.

But this whole chronology of dates changes when you accept that Mahabharata war was around 3067BC and Rama was born in 5114 BC. To reconcile between old and new dates one has to do further research of old scriptures especially Puranas. Firstly one has got to admit that Aryan invasion [1500BC] is a bluff and then secondly, both puranic and Vedic stories need to be put in proper order. We have got to change dates of early Vedic period and late Vedic period from 1750BC---1000BC to much earlier dates in view of new evidence presented. Minimum it could be dated before 3000BC.

Kuru kingdom [74] declined after their defeat by non-Vedic tribes. By 600BC political units Consolidated in to large kingdoms called Mahajanapadas. Process of urbanization began in these Kingdoms. 16 Kingdoms were formed which will be detailed later. By 500BC 4 out of 16 Mahajanpada gained prominence by annexing others. These 4 were Kosala, Magadha, Avanti, and Vatsa. Magadha later has a big role in Indian history.

The end of Vedic India is marked by linguistic, Cultural and political changes. Shramana Movement [including Buddhism, Jainism] challenged Vedic authority later. **Hinduism** evolved over a period of time.

It is quite obvious that Mathematics and science originated in India. From India it went to Arabia and Greece, Persia. Many Rigveda gods like Indra, Mitra, and Varuna find their name in some Persian texts [Zend Avest of Persia]. Theses gods also are seen in seals of treaty between Hittites and Mattani. This shows Vedic influence in Mediterranean prior to Trojan War[75]. There are many Greek gods having similarities with Vedic gods. Indian civilization not only preceded Egyptian, Sumerian civilization but significantly influenced Greece. This Vedic religion with its Rituals and rites got amalgamated in day to day life of Indians and is now known as **Hinduism**. Hinduism is interface between Vedic and local traditions. Dense network of "Tirths" and other holy sites created sacred geography and integrated nation culturally.

Vedic period is not included within historic period of India—hence called protohistoric period. It is wrong to assume Vedic literature talks of religion only. There is enough evidence in Rigveda and Puranas which give us details of Vedic people, how they lived and who ruled them. Vedic hymns were product of various ages. Hymns represented different phases of religion—From multiple gods to single supreme who pervades and governs this universe. Traditional culture of Dravidians tells us that their culture originated from Vedic Aryans.

The mythology of Greeks, Egyptians and Assyrians are founded on Hindu mythology. Ramayana and Mahabharata are sources of

Homeric poems. Even Christian mythology is derived from Hindu mythology. Maurice [89]and Jones[90] believe Rama to be Ramah of scriptures, son of Cush ( genesis, chapter x, verse7). Brown says Hindu is the parent of literature and theology of world. It has been seen that ancient Hindus were neither Idol worshipers nor uncivilized race as depicted in history books.

With all above in mind should n't we say India is start of human civilization. When will West discard Eurocentric attitude to history?

# ANCIENT INDIAN DYNASTIES

British historians believe Alexander's invasion as sheet anchor of Indian history. History prior to 327BC is dismissed. Strabo wrote, "Greek historians were liars". Greek geographers made Alexander to believe that he had reached the end of world after he crossed Persia, such was their ignorance of geography. Defeat of king Porus is yet another lie spread by western writers. Greek writers were making hero of Alexander. Alexander's invasion has been glorified. We Indians should rely on local indigenous evidence than to trust foreign narrative.

Drubbing inconvenient kings as mythological and compressing these rulers in a period of 200-300 years is highly illogical. Aryan invasion theorists want you to believe that Aryans came to India in 1500BC and in just 100 years formed a mighty civilization and fought Mahabharata war in 1400BC - "Highly impossible". These invasionists are at wits end how to fit in various dynasties who ruled India in their time line. Now that this Aryan invasion theory has been rejected, we have to rewrite Indian ancient history taking in account all those kings who ruled

India in ancient past. Puranas and literature especially Rigveda can guide us to put these dynasties in time frame.

Historian Lal[19] puts Krishna in time frame of 5700BC—1400BC with Mahabharata war 3711BC. Prof Achar[30] puts Mahabharata war in 3067BC while Bhatnagar[80] puts Lord Rama in 5114BC and Mahabharata war around 3000BC. Aryabhata [10] puts onset of Kali yug at 3102BC [End of war]. Vartak[29] puts last event of Ramayana at 7292BC and first event of Mahabharata at 5574BC. Gap between two events is 1718 years. These dates coupled with Vayu purana narrative can make us give approximate dates of various dynasties and their ruling time.

According to Vayu purana Pradyota dynasty came into power after killing last king of Brahadarath dynasty. Brahadarath dynasty important king was Jarasandh who figures in Mahabharata war. Now we know Mahabharata war was between 5561BC [Vartak] and 3067BC [Achar]. Brahadarath dynasty must have been ruling around this period only. So, the dates of Pradyota dynasty who ruled for 138 years cannot be 779BC-684BC as given by western historians, dates have got to be much earlier. This Pradyota dynasty was followed by other dynasty rule like, Sisunga, Sunga, Kanava, Haryanka, etc. It may be mentioned here that Haryanka rule was finished by Sisunga. Sinunga also finished Pradyota rule. Dates like 413BC for Sisunga and 779BC for Pradyota are preposterous. From aforesaid one can easily conclude that Brahadarath dynasty must have been ruling anywhere from 5561BC-3067BC.

Rigveda, various Puranas and even EPICS especially Mahabharata [Bhagwat puran] give us graphic details of Kingdoms/janapadas which ruled ancient India. Over 30 janapadas are mentioned in Rigveda and Atharveda. Out of this big list only few survived till 700BC. Kingdoms like Kosala, Kuru and Magdha had a decisive role in shaping India.

Janapadas like Aja, Alina, Anu, Ambastha, Balhika, Bhalana, Bardevaja, Beda, Bodha, Druhyu, Keshin, Kikta, Kirata, Krivi, Kunti, Mahavrisha, Mujavana, Mutiba, Paktha etc had insignificant role in shaping future India.

Some details about significant ancient kingdoms:

## Gandharva Kingdom:

It occupied present day Peshawar and Rawalpindi. Its capital was in Taxila. Taxila is famous for Taxila university. Its name figures in Rigveda. Kingdom, was founded by Ghander who was descendent of Yayati. Vayu purana tells us about destruction of Ghandhar. Ghandhar at certain point was part of Kashmir kingdom. Ghandhara was conquered by Achaemenid empire in600BC, by Alexander in 327BC. Ghandhara had both Hindu and Buddhist influence. King Naganajit of Ghandhara was contemporary of Janaka, king of Videha. Naganjit was defeated by Bharata's son, Taksha who established later Taxila. Ghadhara served as trade centre between India and West. Gandhara is mentioned both in Mahabharata and Ramayana. Ghandhar also became centre for music learning. Its culture survived till 1000BC. Queen Ghandhari of Kurus, Shaukni belonged to this dynasty. Padmasambhva, founder Indo-tibetian Budhhism was from Ghandhar.

**Sindhu Kingdom:**

It was founded by Vrsadarbh, son of Sivi. Its capital was at Vrsadarbh pura, later known as Sindhu. It was located in South Punjab. Its inhabitants were called Sindhu. Word Hindu is a Persian adaptation of word"Sindhu". Persians called Sindhu as Hindus. This kingdom was along Sindhu [indus] river. Harivamsa purana mentions about this kingdom. In Mahabharata war Jayadratha, ruler of Sindh along sauviras and Sivis fought on side of Duryodhana.

Sauviras was small kingdom in lower indus valley. Its capital was Roruka, sauvira founded this kingdom. Sivi kingdom, much smaller had trade relations with Persians, Arabs and Africans. Some Sivi migrated to Yemen and were there known as Sabaeans.

**Madra Kingdom:**

Its capital was Sagla, modern Sialkot. It was founded by son of Yayati, Anu. Aswapti its powerful ruler was father of legendery Savitri. Its another powerful king was Shalya who fought war on Kuru side.

## Kanyakubja Kingdom:

This was part of Drupada kingdom, formed part of southern Panchala. Kingdom was in modern day Kanauj. Jamaaadagni, Vishvamitra were notable in this clan. After defeat by Vasistha, Vishvamitra adopted ascetic life.

## Brahadarath Dynasty -5561BC-3067BC:

This dynasty ruled from Magdha. Its rule started with Somadhi. Descendent of this dynasty was Brihardarth, on whose name this dynasty is named. Brihardarth had a son whose name was Jarasandh. Jarasandh is important character in Mahabharata war. Its last king Rapunjaya was killed by his own minister in 600BC. According to Vayu purana this dynasty ruled for 2600 years. In Mahabharata Brihadratha was placed on throne by Pandavas after duel with Bhima. Puranas tell us Brihadratha was killed by Shaukni. Jarasandha was succeeded by his son Sahadeva who was killed in Kurukhetra war.

## Pradyota Dynasty:

Its rule started from Avanti, present day Madhya Pradesh. According to vayu purana Pradyota conquered Magdha. Rule lasted for 138 years. According to Buddhist and jain texts son killed father and ascended throne in this dynasty. Later people rebelled and put Haryanka on throne. However, Pradyota rule continued till they were conquered by Shisunga. Shisunga later destroyed Haryanka dynasty of Magadh.

## Shisunga Dynasty:

They ruled from Magdha. Capital was Rajgir, later shifted to Patliputra. King Shishunga defeats Haryanka dynasty ruler. He destroyed Pradyota dynasty of Avanti. He spread his wings up to Rajasthan, Sindh, Kandhar, in south up to Madurai and Kochi. Dynasty ruled one of the largest empires of subcontinent. Mahanandin, its last ruler was killed by Mahapadma who founded Nanda empire.

## Haryanka Dynasty:

This dynasty created an area currently known

as Bihar, Jharkhand, West Bengal, Orissa, Bangladesh and part of Nepal. Whole area was called Magdha. Capital was in Rajgir. Its first great ruler, Bimbisara. His wife from Kosala, sister of Parsenjit, ruler of Kosala. He annexed Anga and appointed his son Ajatashatru governor at Champa. He took many wives to strengthen his empire. He was followed by his son, Ajatashatru [494BC-462BC]. Bimbisara was contemporary of Gautam Buddha.

**Shunga Dynasty:**

This was a Brahmin dynasty, Pushymitra started it. He also ruled from Magdha He ruled for 36 years. Dynasty produced 10 kings.

**Kanva Dynasty:**

Vasudeva defeats Devabhuti of Shunga and ascends throne of Magdha. This was also Brahmin dynasty. Later this dynasty was defeated by Satvanaha kings.

**Salva Kingdom:**

This kingdom is grouped amongst western kingdoms in Mahabharata. Sauba was its capital. Legendry Satyavan was from Salwa who married Madra princess, Savitri, daughter of Madra king Aswapti. Salvas were nonvedic tribe, who later invaded Kurukhetra and settled along Yumna river. They adopted Vedic culture. A Salva king, Shalva Kumara is mentioned as lover of Amba, princess of Kashi whom Bhishma abducted for Kuru prince. Another Salwa king, ally of Shishupala attacked Dwarika in absence of Krishna but failed in his mission. A Salwa king even sided with Duryodhana in war.

## Vrishni Kingdom:

Kamsa is tyrant ruler of Vrishni, capital of which is Mathura. Kamsa was son of powerful Yadava king, Ugrasena. He ascends throne after putting his father in prison. He married Jarasandh's daughters. Jarasandh was ruler of Magdha. He loved his sister, Devaki dearly. On hearing heavenly voice that Devaki's 8th son will kill him, he put both Devaki and her husband in prison. He killed Devaki's children one by one. Krishna was saved due to Vasudeva's thinking. Vasudeva during night imports Krishna to Gokul. Years later Krishna kills Kamsa and puts Ugrasena back on throne. Krishna's peace mission to avert war failed. Mahabharata took place on 25<sup>th</sup> oct 3162 BC.

## Kashmir Kingdom:

Our main source of information, Kalhana's Rajtarangni. We are told Kali Yuga started in 3102BC, Pandavas and Kauravas lived at 653 Kali era. Kalhana started his history of Kashmir before Mahabharata war and first king mentioned by him is Gonanda-I. Gonanda-1 ascends throne in Kali samvat653. Length of rule by 75 kings is 2268 years. Gonanda-1 era 3120BC-3103BC. Gonanda was a friend of Jarasandha. Kalhana says king ruled twenty years before Mahabharata war. He was killed by Balrama.

After his death his son, Damodar 1 was installed king. He ruled from 3103-3090BC, succeeded by his wife, Yashomati who ruled for 15 years. She was followed by her son Gonanda-II who ruled for 40 years. He was infant at the time of Great War. He was killed by his PM, Harandev who was from Pandava dynasty. Harandev ruled from 3035BC-3005BC. Harandev was grandson of ARJUN. He went to Kashmir and recruited himself in army of king Gonanda-II. He ruled for 30 years. Last king in this lineage was Gopaldeva who ruled from 2768-2755BC.

## Naga Kingdom:

In MAHABHARATA Naga kingdom is territory of warlike tribe called Nagas. Naga people were serpent worshipers. Nagas are considered ancient Kshatriya tribes of India and had spread all over India. This race was almost killed by Janemejaya, kuru king. Ananta was first among naga kings. Vasuki had kingdom near Kailasa. Takshaka in Takshasila, Nagadeepa in Jaffna, Kalyani in Gampaha is mentioned as their dwellings. Naga king Muchalinda protects Budhha during his penance in forest. Nagas are believed to live in caves or water bodies. Naga Iravan fought in Mahabharata war. He was son of Arjun by Ulupi [naga women]. Mahabharata also talks of naga king, Lohita who ruled close to Kashmir. He was later defeated by Arjuna. According to purana Kashyap's wife Kadroo who belonged to nagas gave birth to the Nagas.

## Pandya Kingdom:

We find their mention in Mahabharata. They were precursors of later big Pandyan empire. Its king Malayadhwaja fought on side of pandavas. He was killed by Ashwatthama. It is said that Pandya king attended swayamwara of Draupdi showing links of southern India with north.

Mahabharata talks of Nishada kingdom. Ekalavya was nishada king. . Nishadas were indigenous tribes.

1. Nanda dynasty----345BC---321BC.

2. Maurya dynasty---321BC---185BC.

In conclusion it is extremely difficult to date ancient dynasties which ruled India. If you belonged to Aryan invasion [1500BC] school then you had to put all these dynasties after 1400BC, date fixed for Mahabharata war by Aryan invasionists, so they put Pradyota dynasty at 779BC-684BC, Haryanka at 544BC, SHISUNGA at 413BC, Sunga at 185BC and so on. Now that this invasion theory stands debunked and Mahabharata war date has gone beyond 3000BC, dates of these dynasties need to be rewritten. That is why Brihadratha dynasty is now dated somewhere in between 5561BC---3067BC. Since Pradyota followed Brihadaratha its dates should be somewhere near Brihardartha, rest of the ruling dynasties could be dated accordingly. We are reasonably sure about dates of Nanda dynasty and Maurya dynasty as by that time writing/documentation had got perfected.

In South India we had Pandya dynasty ruling in 550BC, Chola and Chera in 300BC and Satvanaha dynasty ruling 271BC.

It is necessary here to mention a few words about solar dynasty and Lunar dynasty as they have important role in ancient India history.

## Solar Dynasty:[27]

This dynasty is also called Suryavansh. Dynasty starts with Manu vivasvata who is 7th Manu in order. His eldest son was Ishvaku. He founded the dynasty around 8000BC. Raja Harishchandra, Bhagiratha, Dilipa, Raghu, Ajas belong to this dynasty. Ajas was father of Dashratha, who was father of Lord Rama. Rama is believed to be 7th avatar of Lord Vishnu. Rishi Vashishta was preceptor of this dynasty. Puranas give details of all the kings of this dynasty. King Bridbhala of this dynasty was killed by Abhimanyu in Mahabharata war. Brihadbala was 116th king of this dynasty. After Brihadbala there are 31 kings in this dynasty. Last king was Sumitra. Lord Rama was 67th king of this dynasty. Buddhists and Jain texts also give chronology of kings in this dynasty with some variations. Bhatnagar dates Lord Rama around 5114BC.

**Lunar Dynasty:**[44]

According to Mahabharata Ila was dynasty's progenitor. Purva founded this dynasty. Shantanu, son of Pratipa was kuru king who ruled from Hastinapur. Shantanu was descendent of Bharata, son of Dushyant and Shakuntala. Shantanu was common ancestor of Kuru and Pandva. King Parakshit and Janemaja belong to this dynasty. Kuru dynasty is involved in famous Mahabharata war. After war king Parakshit takes charge of kingdom when Yudhishtra abdicates throne. Mahabharata war, Lord Krishna, Bhagwat Gita all belong to this dynasty. Mahabharata war dates fall between 5561BC [Vartak][29] to 3067BC [Achar][30].

Variation in dates by different authors is due to different tools used to arrive at conclusion. But one thing is dead certain that dates are much earlier than 1500BC given by western writers. These western writers want to negate India's ancient glorious past for some obvious reasons.

# KINGDOMS AND MAHAJANPADAS

## Mahajanpadas [52, 76, 77]

Historical records show that there were 16 kingdoms in ancient India [1000BC—600BC] [76, 77]. Mahajanapadas took shape after tribal organizations reorganized themselves and formed Janapadas [States]. Each Janapadas tried to dominate other. In this process of reorganization Democracy was replaced by Kingship. Sixteen Janapadas which took shape were as follows:

1. Kashi: Capital was in present Banaras. It covered area of present day Varanasi. Kashi vishwanath is famous temple of this area. Kashi kingdom was founded by Khsetravridha, the son of Ayus. Eventually Kashi merged with Kosala. Stories tell us struggle for supremacy between Kashi and three other kingdoms of Kosala, Angaand Magdha. Kashis find mention in vedic texts. Even today kashi Naresh is revered by people. Kingdom lost its independence in1194. Residential place of Naresh is Ram Nagar fort. Ram Lila recounting Lord Rama

story is performed for 31 days, based on Ramchritmanas of Tulsi das.

2. Panchala: This covered Gangetic Uttar Pradesh with its capital at Kampila. Kanauj is important town of kingdom. Kannauj became Centre of higher studies, art and culture of this mahajanpada. All tribes of Panchala are descendants from Dushmanta and parameshthin. Panchala was divided into south and north. Draupad ruled south, while north was ruled by Ashwathama, son of Drona. kurus were exiled after defeat by Panchalas. Later Kuru retook capital. Bharata prince Samvarana was defeated by panchalas. Bharata was reinstated later by Vasishtha. Kurus and Panchalas were considered foremost among ruling tribes in ancient India.

3. Surasena: Its capital was at Mathura. This place was strong hold of Yadvas. Lord Krishna is associated with this place.

4. Malla: This mahajanpada covered Eastern Uttar Pradesh with capital at Kushinara. This janapada is mentioned in Buddhist and Jain texts also. Mahabharata talks of Bhima

defeating chief of Mallas during his expedition to east.

5. Matasya: This mahajanpada covered areas of Rajasthan [Jaipur, Alwar]. Viratnagri was its capital.

6. Kuru: This covered areas of present Haryana Punjab and Delhi, had its capital at Hastinapur. This Janapada ruled for long period and was involved in great Mahabharata war.

7. Kosala: This mahajanpada covered areas of present Uttar radesh [FAIZABAD] area]. This kingdom is involved with solar dynasty, Lord Rama and epic Ramayana. Ishvaku founded it.

8. Avanti: This covered central India [Malwa region], had capital at Ujjain. Its famous king was Vikramaditya. This king is known for valor and intelligence. Avanti finds its mention in Mahabharata. It was later merged with Magdh. Avanti kings Vinda and Anuvinda fought for Duryodhyana in war. They were killed by Arjuna.

9. Vatsa: Capital at Kaushambi, covered areas of present Uttar Pradesh [Allahabad].

They were off shoots of Kuru. Udayana was its ruler in 600BC, at the time of Budhha.

10. Gandhara: Taxila was its capital, covered Afghanistan and parts of present Rawalpindi.

11. Kamboj: Its capital was at Rajpura, covered parts of Kashmir [Poonch area]. It was located around Hindu kush region of Kashmir. In Ramayana it is recorded that Kamboja's joined Vasistha during battle of kamdhenu against king Vishvamitra of Kanauj. Mahabharata talks of Kamboj settlements in Hindu kush. Kambojs and Gandhars never came in contact with Magdha till Chandergupt Maurya arrived on scene, Puranas talk of war of Kambojs with Sagara. Rajtarangni talks of King Lalita ditya annexing Kamboj in800AD,

12. Magadha: Rajgir was its capital. This janapada covered areas of Bihar [Patna, Gaya]. Its famous rulers were Bimbisara, Ajatshatru. Greatest of all kingdoms was Magdha. It finds its mention in Ramayana, Mahabharata, puranas and in jain and Buddhist texts. Maurya and Gupta empire originated in Magdha, saw advancements in science, math, astronomy, religion and

philosophy. Its first ruler was Brihadratha. King Bimbisara of Haryanka dynasty led a expansive policy. It was most prosperous state of its times. Existence of Magdha is recorded in Atherveda also. Core of kingdom included Bihar and Bengal. Magdha annexed Anga and Vajji confederations. It had belief of its own. Magdha had sramana traditions--- did not worship Vedic deities. Sought freedom from birth cycle through spiritual knowledge. Importance of Magdha can be seen in that Buddhism, Jainism and Hinduism adopted some of its features, significantly a belief of rebirth.

13 Chedi: This covered areas of present day Bundelkhand, had capital at Shuktimati. Chedi had role in Mahabharata time. Its king Sishupal was killed by Krishna. Chedi kings mainly kalinga belt.

14. Vajji: This covered areas of Bihar and Uttar Pradesh with capital at Vaishali. It was a confederation of nine clans [Lichchhavi, Videhans, Inatrikas were main]. Videhas kingdom had its capital at Mithila. Its most powerful king was Janaka. Brihadaranyaka Upanishad mentions Janaka, a great

philosopher Sita was from Videha. Later this kingdom merges with Vriji.

15. Anga: This covered parts of Bihar [Bhagalpur area], capital at Champa. Vanga kingdom was near present day Bengal. In Mahabharata we are told they paid tributes to Yudhishtra. Mahabharata mentions Anga and Vanga as forming one kingdom. These kingdoms later got merged withMagdha. Even Ramayana mentions Anga as a place connected to Kamdeva death. Duryodhana made Karna, king of Anga. The founders of Anga, Vanga, Kalinga, Pundras and Suhmas had common ancestry. Vangas sided with Duryodhana in war.

16. Assaka: This covered parts of southern Maharashtra, capital wasat Potana.

Out of 16 mahajanpadas only 4 continued by 500BC-600BC. These 4 were Kosala, Avanti, Vatsa and Magadha. They were either monarchies or republics. Their language was Sanskrit. It is interesting to note that all these Kingdoms [Janapadas] which are bracketed in history between 1000BC-600BC] have roots much beyond [3000 BC—4000BC. Nearly all of them are mentioned in Rigveda, Atharveda, Ramayana and Mahabharata. It means history dates we are told [1000BC-600BC] are wrong. These Janapadas existed in ancient India [3000BC-4000BC] with ups and downs. It also means they are historical, not mythological. This clearly shows India had a meaningful civilization long before Sumeria, Egypt and Greece.

Now we will talk in some detail about only two dynasties, Kuru and Kosala as these are connected with two great Indian epics, Ramayana and Mahabharata.

**Kuru kingdom78**

Kuru was name of Aryan tribe in northern India. By 1200—850BC area developed in to state level society. Area became dominant political and cultural Centre during reign of King Parikshit and king Janamejaya but declined in importance by 500BC. Kuru ruled Ganga-Jumna doab including modern Haryana. Kuru tribe was formed by merger of Bharata clan with Puru clan and was a dominant force from 1200BC—800BC. Its capital was in Hastinapur but later shifted to Indraprastha, which falls in modern Delhi.

Parkshit and his son Janamajaya were its famous rulers. Kuru's decline started with its defeat by Panchalas and capital shifted to Kaushambi.

To aid king in governance priests developed a new set of rituals to uphold social order and strengthen class hierarchy. Horse sacrifice was a way for powerful king to assert his dominance. Epic" Mahabharata" tells of conflict between two clans of Kurus. Mahabharata war, historical basis [some doubt] is dated from1000BC—to 3067BC by different writers depending on the tools they applied to arrive at dates. Kurus were successful in governing whole of northern India. Holy Bhagwat Geeta is byproduct of this Mahabharata war between two clans [cousins].

**Kosala Kingdom**[79]

Ayodhya was capital of Kosala kingdom. Its founder was king Ikshavaku. Lord **Rama** is from same lineage. Whole epic Ramayana revolves around Lord Rama from his birth to kingship which follows after defeat of Lankan king Ravana. Two sons of Lord Rama ruled different areas. Lava ruled from city which was called Stravasti and Kusa from Kushvati. A colony of Kosala rajahs existed in present Madhya Pradesh which was called Dakshina Kosala.

. Lord Rama's influence extended from north of India to South including Lanka. He had good relations with southern kingdoms, Kishkanda was one of them. Brother of Lord Rama Bharata colonized and founded Takshilla, Laxman founded Laxmanpura, present day Lucknow, and Shatrughna founded Mathura after destroying forest king Madhu. Details of this solar dynasty from its founder to King Parsenjit, who is mentioned in Mahabharata, are to be seen in Puranas. The King not only offered protection but lived himself by example. There was no border security those days. A defeated king was asked to pay one time tribute and would be invited to sacrifice ceremony. New kingdoms were formed when a major Clan produced more than one king in generation. Kosala kingdom was later absorbed in Magadha Kingdom.

# ARE LORD RAMA AND LORD KRISHNA HISTORICAL?

There have systemic attempts by western writers to label Ramayana and Mahabharata epics with no historicity. Divinity is definitely a matter of faith but historicity is proof of one's existence. If Lord Rama and Lord Krishna were not historical, how come we have existence of places and traditions mentioned in Ramayana and Mahabharata even today after a gap of over 5000 years? What about Ramsetu which is being dated by some 5076BC? What about submerged Dwarika city located in Gujarat [Rao].

James Mills and Charles Grant who were assigned to write history of India never visited India. Their sole purpose was to tell students that India had no civilization and its literature is a fabricated trash. This they wrote despite there being existence of voluminous literature of Vedic Period. Whole idea was to discredit India. Al Birauni writes in 1030AD about Lord Rama and Ramsetu. Akbar Ramayana 1588AD writes about historicity of Lord Rama. Research done by

Sri Lankan government has shown that there is evidence of king Ravana's palace and other Places mentioned in Ramayana. This gives credence of theory that Lord Rama was a historical Figure.

If we do a serious study of Bhagwat Puran and other related literature, one can make reasonable guess of events as mentioned in Epic Ramayana. In Bhagwat while describing an event position of stars is clearly mentioned. Let us do convergence in literature, archeology and local traditions and we can easily find facts. For example, it is mentioned that prince Bharata while travelling from Kaikeyi to Ayodhya crossed river Sarasvati. This river has dried up nearly 3000BC. Other rivers mentioned in text are present in same order even today. This should give us time frame of Bharata's travel. Ancient Indian's used stars as clock and position of stars while describing a historical event. MR P. Bhatnagar[80] while publishing his book, "Dating the era of lord Rama".

Using planetarium software has come out with following dates:

1. Birth of Lord Rama --10th January, 5114BC

2. Coronation ------------ 4th January, 5089BC

3. Khar dushan encounter ------------- 5077BC

4. Megnath killed --------------- Nov. , 5076BC

5. War ------------------------ 20th Sep 5076BC

6. Hanuman meets Sita ---------- 12. 9. 5076BC

Author used the method which he calls Archeo-astronomy. To account for discrepancy in birth date which falls on Chetra Navmi author says for every 72 years one day is to be added [astrological correction/ necessity]. Professor Achar of Memphis University using star positions as mentioned in Bhagwat has come out with date of Mahabharata war---3067BC[81.] It is true we don't have relics of this period.

Reason for this is huge time gap from today, oral transmission, and writing came late, vandalism by later rulers etc. One relic of Ramayana time is Ramsetu, bridge between India and Sri Lanka. Its Presence has been established by satellite photos. Al -Baruni 1030AD mentions about this foot bridge existing between India and Lanka. This got submerged in sea as late as 1480AD. Ramsetu is mentioned in Ramayana as 100 Yojanas in length and 10 Yojanas in width. As on today this Submerged Bridge is 35Km in length and 3. 5 Km in breadth. This ratio of 1:10 is not just Coincidence but another proof of its existence in ancient past. Even past Jaffna kings minted Coins with word Setu embossed in it. Its unique curvature indicates it is manmade and not a geographical occurrence. Land on both sides of bridge is geographically dated 1, 750, 000 years Old. Ram Setu is being dated 5076BC.

It is interesting to note that Rama veneration was not confined to India alone but spread to Far East, Thailand, Malaysia, Indonesia, Cambodia. In Thailand king still takes title of Rama.

If Rama were not a historical figure, how come veneration outside India would be possible?

When we look at Solar dynasty, of which clan Lord Rama belonged, we see 51 kings preceded him and 32 followed him of his dynasty. Last ruler of solar dynasty was Bridbala who was killed by Abhimanyu in Mahabharata war. Valmiki has written biography of Lord Rama in Rama's time only; later writers have added lot of material to the book but retained basic story. Historian, B. B. LAL[82] dates Lord Krishna any time between 5700BC—1400BC. Kalhana dates Mahabharata war in 2449BC. As per Saptarishis calendar Mahabharata war is dated3711BC.

Sanderson Beck[83] in his book "Literature of India" gives time frame of 12000—10000 years for Ramayana and Mahabharata. Pilny and Arrian Greek historians have identified 154 kings from Lord Rama to Chandra Gupta Maurya [321BC] There are writers who say between king Parikshit and Nanda dynasty over 1050 years elapsed. Ishvaku founder of solar dynasty is reported to have ruled in 8000BC. Last king of this dynasty was

Sumitra who was ousted by Nanda in 400BC[84.] Rajaraman and Frawley[85] date Mahabharata 3000BC. From these above mentioned dates it becomes obvious that Lord Rama and Krishna were historical figures. Different dates by different by writers could be due to tools they used to determine the dates.

Coins of Lord Krishna and Balarama have been found in Kabul [date 300BC]. Submerged Dwarika city has been found of Gujarat coast, dated between 1500BC, a pillar was erected by Heliodors in honour of Lord Krishna speaks of Krishna as person not as myth. Two submerged cities, 150feet deep in water have been carbon dated, 7500— 12000 year near Gujarat, possibly coinciding with end of Ice age. Even tools, fossilized vertebrates, Pottery, Jewelry have been found of theses submerged cities. This speaks of their existence. Places mentioned in Mahabharata and Ramayana are still present in India. A holy inscription of king Pulakeshin1 of Badami mentions Of Mahabharata war in 3131BC. Cunningham explored Kurukshetra and was able to demarcate Land where war was fought. Continued oral and living traditions along with places authenticate historicity of Mahabharata. Maues, an indoscythian king 85BC besides worshiping Greek gods was also worshiping Krishna. Krishna and Balarama worship is seen in stone graffiti of Chilas Caves in western Pakistan [200BC]. Panini [600BC] writes about Vasudeva and Arjun in his Sutra [4. 3. 98]. Mahaummagga Jatka [300BC] writes about Krishna. Even Patanjali [150BC] in Mahabhashva praises Krishna and Balarama. Chhandogya Upanishad [3. 17. 6] composed around 900BC mentions about Krishna. When we agree Kalyuga started in 3102BC then Krishna can be easily dated between 3300BC—3200BC[86]. Mahabharata mentions that Balarama went from Dwarika to Mathura to immerse ashes in Ganges by navigating river Saraswati. Since river dried up by 1900BC and was navigable in Balarama time then date of Krishna can be easily fixed around 3000BC[16]. Even Jain literature profusely mentions Krishna. Ghata Jatka [300BC] talk of Krishna as ruler.

Can we ignore all above evidence plus continued tradition just to please self-styled Indologists who talk of Aryan invasion, a theory now debunked?

In conclusion we can say with authority that both Lord Rama and Lord Krishna were historical figures. Their stories have got blended with Puranic stories and local legends of time. Then some writers added their own materials to immortalize the characters. By this involuntarily they blurred historical image of their characters. It is pertinent to mention here that basic story of Epic Ramayana and Mahabharata has remained same in all books despite repeated additions and alterations. We cannot ignore archeological finds, Astronomical data, and carbon dating, Satellite imagery and continued traditions just because of some fantasy in Puranic stories. If they were not historical there would have been no temples to venerate them? Why there are no temples for thousands of heroes/characters mentioned in Puranas, reason they were not historical?

# VEDIC LITERATURE

Despite there being voluminous literature of this Vedic civilization, it is nearly ignored by west. Western writers labeled it full of myth and also called it trash. West would not accept that east is Cradle of human civilization because of their superiority complex. It stands even genetically Proved that Europe which has U and U5a genes has its origins in India. But there are some Scholars though in minority who acknowledge India's past greatness.

Arab scholar SaidIbn Ahmad al-Andalusi said, " First nation to have cultivated science is India, whether it was Trigonometry, Calculus, Medicine, Metallurgy or Astronomy. Most of the advances in sciences that we consider today to have been made in Europe were in fact made in India centuries ago".

J. T. Sunderland said, " India created beginnings of all American science writers and she carried some of them to a remarkable degree of development.......... ."

Louis Jacolliot, French scholar said, " Hindu revelation [Vedas] is of all revelations, the only whose ideas are in perfect harmony with modern science, as it proclaims the slow and gradual formation of world. "

Carl Sagan, astrophysicist commented, " The Hindu religion is the only one of the great faiths, dedicated to the idea that Cosmos itself under goes an immense, indeed, an infinite number of deaths and births. It is only religion in which time scales correspond to those of modern Cosmology".

Vedic civilization evolved over a period of time and gave birth to a religious philosophy called Sanataan Dharma, now known **Hinduism**. This religion did not come on a particular day but evolved over a time. Ancient Indian literature is in two forms: Shruti---means what is heard and Smriti--- means what is remembered. Vedas come under category of Shrutis while Ramayana and Mahabharata and Manu Smriti come under Smritis category. Shrutis literature is veritable and **inviolable**. On contrary Smriti literature may get modified under influence of time and place.

Smriti literature has its basis in Shruti.

Vedas constitute sublime knowledge revealed to Rishi's while doing penance. Vedas are eternal. They acquired verbal form during certain point in history. They are timeless in the sense that they are beyond the confines of time. Vedas contain divine knowledge. They are earliest document of human mind. They encompass human life and they do not belong to any race or Country. They reflect all aspects of existence. They throw light on **Creation**, **Atman** and all related issues of spiritualism. Vedas contain mantras which have different and specific purposes. Vedas are **laconic** in form and hardly intelligible without interpretation. These books are products of man's contemplation and God's revelation. No dogma is allowed to come in way.

Word Veda originates from word "**VID**" i. e. "to know". Ved Vyasa categorized and compiled all Mantras in 4 parts, called 4 Vedas. Mantras are in form of metered verses. Vedas acquired written form very late. Of the 4 Vedas [Rig, Sam, Yajur and Athar], Rigveda is the oldest. Some Scholars say Vedas have two parts---Brahmanas and

Samhitas while others believe that Vedas have four parts, namely- Brahmanas, Samhitas, Aranyakas and Upanishads. Samhitas and Brahmanas constitute rites and rituals while Aranyakas and Upanishads constitute" **Gyan Khand**". Brahmanas hint at magical power of sacrificial rituals. Samhitas deal with nature and Deities. In Aranyakas spiritual interpretation of rituals and ceremonies is evident. Upanishads are Concluding part of Vedas. Upanishads are in form of dialogue, contain sublime knowledge that deals with the topic at great depth. There are 108 Upanishads. Among these Katha, Chhandogya, Isha andMundaka are highly popular. Main message of all Upanishads is to get awareness of Atman. All Upanishads say Atman [Soul] is imperishable but body is perishable. Atman is real and is veiled by karma. By meditation this veil can be removed and true nature of Atman perceived. By and large Upanishad teachings are spiritual and other worldly.

Next piece Vedic literature are Puranas. Puranas deal with Creation, cosmology and history of times. Broadly puranas are categorized under three headings—Vishnu Puran, Shiv Puran and Brahm Puran. All puranas fall under these three heads. Puranas are supplementary explanations of Vedas.

**Hindu philosophy**:

Continuity of Indian culture which is over 5000years old lies in its spiritual foundations. Philosophy rose as an enquiry into mysteries of life and existence. These enquires were carried in the inner world unlike Greeks who confined it to external world. Sages found Atman is unchangeable while body is changeable. Atman is true source of man. Sages found this Atman [soul] is part of Paratman [GOD]. Hindu philosophy evolved over a period of time taking full advantage of Vedas and Upanishads. Six schools of philosophy took birth in a span of 1000 years. These six schools are: Nyaya, Vaisheshika, Mimamsa, Samkhya, Yoga and Vedanta. Modern exponents of Vedanta philosophy were Adi Shankara charya and Swami Vivekananda.

Besides above philosophies Vedic literature gave us two epics---Ramayana, Mahabharata and Bhagwat Gita. Bhagwat Gita can be called summary of Vedic [Upanishad] wisdom.

Entire Vedic tradition presents conclusion than beginning of literary activity. Vedas are seldom read now a days but they form bedrock of the Sanatan Dharma [**Hinduism**]. All rituals from birth to death owe their origins in Vedas. Besides 4 major Vedas there are minor one's dealing with different topics. These minor Vedas go by name of Vedanges and Upveda.

French philosopher, Roman Rolland said, "If there is a place on the face of this earth where all dreams of living men have found a home from the very earliest days when man began the dreams of existence, it is India. "

# INDIA'S CONTRIBUTION TO WORLD

## Atomic theory [87, 88]:

Modern science gives credit to Dalton for atomic theory. Instead father of this theory is Rishi Kashyapa also called Kanada. Kashyapa lived around 600BC. He was first to tell that Atom is indestructible and also gave theory of Gravity [Gurutva] long before Isaac Newton. He also said all living beings are made of 5 elements [water, fire, earth, ether, air]. Details of his work can be got from Vaisheshika sutra. He further said atoms can be in two states: -- rest, in motion. This theory of atoms is enmeshed in philosophy.

## Medicine:

Two seers Charaka and Sushrata did pioneering work in this field long before present medical science. Charaka who lived around 600 BC [some say 300BC] wrote treatises on human embryology, diseases of heart, Diabetes, T. B. He also wrote on hundreds of herbs, their medicinal value. Many of the herbs mentioned in Charak

Samhita are in use even today. Samhita also deals in physiology, Embryology, concepts of digestion, metabolism and immunity. Sushrata, who lived around same period, wrote on nearly 300 surgical procedures like Caesarean, Cataract, Urinary stones, Rhinoplasty etc. His work on Rhinoplasty is being quoted by plastic surgeons even today. He alsoWrote on various suture materials and surgical instruments. He used horse hair as Suturing material.

## Aviation Technology:

Saint Bhardawaja, who reportedly lived around 800BC not only wrote Atharveda but also wrote on Aviation science, flying machines, and space science in Yantra Sarvasva. One can easily say that ancient people living in India were aware of flying machines. In his book, saint discusses various types of Flying machines. Sage mentions in his book that 500 types of vimanas can be made. In 1895AD Shiv Kumar Talpade was first person in world to fly a Plane, long before Wright brothers.

## Creation:

Saint Kapila can easily be labeled as father of cosmology. He said Prakriti with Inspiration from Purusha forms this Universe. He gave Samkhya philosophy detailing how this world that we see was formed. This philosophy is also quoted in Holy Bhagavat Gita. HE wrote in great detail on Primal matter and process of Creation long before Big Bang theory was proposed by modern science. Kapila is reported to have lived around 3000BC[75]

## Planetaty System:

Bhaskara in his book Siddhant Shiroman talks of planetary positions, Eclipses,

Cosmography and Gravity. He lived in 12th century. Varahimira [499AD-587AD]Writes in Surya Siddhanta about constellations, geography. He also wrote on animal science. Aryabhata [476AD] wrote first time that Earth is round, rotates on its axis, orbits Sun, and 1000 years before Copernicus. He also gave Trigonometry, Decimal system, calculating Pi up to 4 decimals, Zero Algebra, quadratic equation to name a few out of his wide contribution to science of mathematics. He also said circumference of Earth is 4967

Yojanas and diameter 1581 I/24 Yojanas. Since 1 Yojanas=5 miles, it gave Circumference of Earth as 24835 miles [24902 miles is accepted by science today].

He also said orbits of planets are ellipses. Copernicus and Galileo came much later who west thinks are founders of Astronomy. It was Aryabhata who fixed seven days for a week. Besides zero Aryabhata gave numerals also. Binomial theorem also given by Aryabhata. It is interesting to know here that West learnt about numerals from Arabs but Arabs themselves called these numerals as Indian and called Indian math as Indian Art. West does not acknowledge this. This shows amount of prejudice west had against India. Decimal and place value system also given by Aryabhata. Without Zero binary system computer application would have been impossible.

Great Einstein said about India, "We owe a lot to the Indians who taught us how to Count without which no worthwhile scientific discovery could have been made. "

• **Nagarjuna** [100AD] discusses Subject of and Metallurgy and chemistry.

• **Patanjali** [200BC] developed science of Yoga, wrote a treatise on Kundalini Shakti and how to awaken it. He asserted that control of breath will lead to control of mind and senses.

• **Panini** in 600 BC gave grammar for Sanskrit language. Sanskrit is only language

Which is computer compatible. It has over 100 million words, highest for any language.

• **Vatsayana** who lived in Gupta empire time wrote Kama sutra giving 64 ways of love making for husband and wife.

• **Budhyana** in 1500BC gave concept of what goes by name of Pythagoras theorem nowadays.

• **Art** of Navigation was known to Indus – Saraswat people way back in 2500BC. Indus People were first to construct dams and build water reservoirs way back in 2000BC.

• Integral calculus was invented by Madhvachaya and differential calculus by

Baskaracharya. His book "leelavati" discusses Vedic math. Vedic math has 17 sutras.

All calculations and mathematical problems can be solved by knowing these sutras.

• **Brahmgupta** gave addition, subtraction, multiplication and division concepts.

• **Ice making** was known to Indians as early as 600AD, time of king Harsh

• **Pape**r making from grass and making of battery.

• **Coins** were made by Indus valley people way back in 2000BC

• **Zinc** making was known in India in 1300AD. Charak Samhita tells us about mercury.

• **Steel** making technology was available in 1795AD.

. Diamond mining originate from India.

**First University** in world was in Takshilla in700BC, Followed by Nalanda in 400BC. Students came also from neighboring countries. Nearly 10, 000 students were reading in theses Universities. Subjects taught were Vedas, Languages, Grammar, Medicine, Surgery, Politics, Astronomy, Commerce, Math, Mystic science etc. Chinese traveler Hien Tsang mentions in his book that Nalanda University had 200 Professors and had 10, 000 students on roll.

• Till 1896, India only country which was source of Diamonds.

• **Chess board** and cards invented in India.

• **God particle** [Higgs boson]. Bose was first to predict God particle followed by Higgs.

• **Crescograph:** To measure growth in plants invented by j. Bose in early 20th century.

• **Dockyard** was used by Indus people in 3000BC. They were first to make buttons from sea shells and used them. Rulers were made from ivory. Dentistry was known to Indus valley civilization.

• **Indian ink**, bow drill to drill gem stones known since 400BC.

• World famous **Damascus** sword from Syria used in wars had steel got from India.

• **Sanskrit**: --- Sanskrit is mother of all languages. Forbes magazine reported Sanskrit is Computer friendly.

. **Dry cell:** Saint Agastya invented it before Christian era. He also told us how to split water in to hydrogen and oxygen in Agastya Samhita. He is founder of Tamil language.

**Charak Samhita** tells us about **Mercury** and its usage.

CIVIL engineering found its manifestation in construction of Temples, Palaces and Fortes. Science of ship building and navigation was known. Maccha yantra [Fish machine] was used as compass by mariners.

It is quite obvious from above that Indian people in ancient times were quite ahead of times. They not only developed a full-fledged civilization but continued their research for Truth both in outer world and inner world and had a reasonable success too. They had sound knowledge of science especially of Math. and Astronomy. Their pursuit for Truth, without any dogmas led to evolution of various Hindu **philosophies**.

Grant Duff, British historian, who said "Many of the advances in science that we consider today to have been made in Europe were in fact made in India centuries ago".

Arnold Toynbee, Historian, "It is becoming clearer that a chapter which has western beginning will have to have an Indian ending if it is not to end in self-destruction of the human race.... . At this Supremely dangerous movement in history the only way of salvation for mankind is the Indian way".

# HINDU ANTIQUITY: TIME FRAME

It is beyond doubt now that Hinduism [Vedic religion] is oldest religion in world. Its past is intricately associated with local traditions making it difficult for scholars to date events. Hidden in its depths are traces of early religion on this earth but lost to history. Indologists who invented Migration theory [1500BC] totally ignored its traditional history before 1500BC. Now that this Imaginary migration theory has been debunked by many scholars, an attempt is being made to rewrite India's past especially before 1500BC. It is interesting to note that we have lots of archeological finds of Indus Valley Civilization but no written material. On contrary we have tons of literature of Vedic civilization but archeological documents are missing. One possible reason could be huge time gap between today and of the antiquity events. One has to rewrite India's ancient history taking in to account, Puranic stories, Epics, other literary material available and corroborate it with Astronomical data, Satellite imagery, Traditional history,

Continued traditions and if needed genetic data also can be included. Archeological data alone cannot suffice. It is only then we can arrive at reasonable conclusion.

Various scholars have used different parameters in rewriting India's past and dating the events.

Following is the summary of conclusions of some scholar's vis-à-vis chronology of events:

Table 1 [86], Rajaram:

| 35, 000-10, 000 BC | Paleolithic Ages |
| --- | --- |
| 6000-5000 BC | Beginning of Indus valley civilization and Vedic civilization |
| 3700 BC | Battle of 10 kings |
| 3100 BC | Incarnation of Lord Krishna |
| 2000-1500 BC | End of Indus civilization |

Table 2:

| Date | Event | Source |
| --- | --- | --- |
| 8000 BC | No indication of invasion seen | Gupta [archeologist] |
| 8000-4000 BC | Vedic civilization | Tilak |
| 7000-6500BC | Indus valley civilization | Chandler |
| 6500-3100BC | Early Vedic-Harappa | Frawley |
| 6000 BC | Rig Veda | Tilak |
| 5114 BC | Rama birth | Bhatnagar |
| 5076 BC | Rama-Ravan War | Bhatnagar |
| 4500-2000 BC | Vedic civilization flourished | Jacobi |
| 3676 BC | Kalyuga | Spat Rishi calendar |

| 3100-1900BC | Period of Vedas | Frawley |
|---|---|---|
| 3067 BC | Mahabharata war | Achar |
| 1900-1000BC | End of Vedas/ Harappa civilization | Frawley |
| 3676 BC | Start Saptrishi calender | |

Table 3:

| 12000-10000 BC | Ramayana and Mahabharata | Sanderson beck |
|---|---|---|
| 9676 BC | Ramayana | Saptarishis/Yuga calendar |
| 6000 BC | Indo-Europeans | Renfrew |
| 5700-1400 BC | Date for Krishna | Lal |
| 4300 BC | Zodiac discussed and dated | Dharampal |
| 3711 BC | Mahabharata war | Lal |
| 3137 BC | Mahabharata war | Pulakeshin1 |
| 3102 BC | Kalyuga | Aryabhata |

| | | |
|---|---|---|
| 3067 BC | Mahabharata war | Achar |
| 2449 BC | Mahabharata war | Varahimira |
| 1400 BC | Mahabharata war | Pusalkar |
| 950 BC | Mahabharata war | Pargiter |

In August 1995, 43 historians and Archeologists fixed Mahabharata war between 3139BC—3138BC. There are scholars who say Indian civilization must be seen unbroken and they have pushed back dates to 7000BC—8000BC.

Table 4

| 1 | Ram janam | 29th Nov, 12240 B. C |
| 2 | Ram banvas | 20th Dec, 12223 B. C. |
| 3 | Bali YUD | 22nd Sept, 12210 B. C. |
| 4 | Hanuman ln Lanka | 27th Aug, 12209 B. C. |

According to Oak RAMAYANA PERIOD 12209 BC and Mahabharata 5561BC. He believes war started on Amavasya [Margashirsa Shukla PAKHS] and Dwarka was flooded 36 years after Mahabharata war. This flood is corroborated by geological event at that time. He used Astronomy, Mahabharata chronology and geological events to the time frame he mentions in his book. These dates are at variance with Bhatnagar who used Astronomy as a tool in his research.

# CONCLUSION

Word Arya means people living by ideals, postulated by Vedas. It does not refer to any race or Language. It is proved beyond doubt that imaginary Aryan invasion of India was biggest Intellectual bluff spread by western writers to undermine indigenous Vedic civilization of India. Concept of people, language and Agriculture arriving in India together through Northwest corridor does not hold up to scrutiny.

It also has been conclusively proved that European genes U, U5a are derivatives of gene N which originated in India. M17 as a marker for Aryan invasion also stands disapproved. M17 has been seen in tribal groups in South which also undermines it as a marker for invasion. Scholars have suggested that M17 could have gone from India through Kashmir, then Central Asia and then to Europe [67, 70].

After failing with Invasion theory scientifically and archeologically [no invasion finds] then Eurocentric scholars shifted their stance to Linguistic invasion. Chief proponent of this was MaxMuller who initially had mooted idea of Aryan invasion. This change of stance was due his self-Interests and for political reasons. Aryan invasion theory was created by European writers to free themselves from Jewish heritage of Christianity. It was as a tool of propaganda to show Superiority of west and legitimize occupation. Even this linguistic theory met same fate as Invasion theory. Nowhere on this earth is Sanskrit spoken or known except in India. There is no mention of Sanskrit in Central Asia or nearby areas. Veda as literature is not only in India but there is continued practice of its rites and rituals in India even today. Mention of word, " Aryaputra" at so many places in Epics suggests nobility and not race. This Vedic civilization was Indigenous and later it had its influence in Iran, Europe and South East Asia.

India has been cradle of human civilization. Vedic culture gave birth to a religion called Sanatan Dharma [Hinduism]. This religion evolved over a period of time. Hinduism does not demand blind faith but pursuit of Truth through dharma traditions [Controlling mind]. This religion unlike other religions has no single founder, no linear history and no single canon to follow. Its solution to pluralism is far superior to Abrahamic religions. Vedas are foundation of Sanatan Dharma [Hinduism]. Religion in India is meant way of life which enabled man to realize true nature.

When philosophy provided reality, religion showed correct way of life.

Word Veda means self-knowledge---"Knowing one's own nature". It has two types of Literature: Shruti and Smriti. Shruti literature is veritable and inviolable. On contrary Smriti Literature may get modified with time. Vedas constitute sublime knowledge revealed to Rishi's while doing penance. They encompass human life and they do not belong to any race. They reflect all aspects of Existence. Vedas are timeless and eternal. They throw light on Creation, Atman and all related issues of spiritualism. Veda philosophy is focused on Jagat [universe]. Veda knowledge is experienced and then recited in Hymns. This Vedic knowledge initially was transmitted orally as writing came late. Holy Bhagvad Gita is essence of Vedas. Vedic knowledge tells us Jiva [man] is trapped in this universe due to his Karma. Moksha is goal of Life, unlike Christianity where goal is freedom in Paradise [Heaven]. Purpose of Bhagavad Gita Is to spread esoteric knowledge to mankind, knowledge difficult to get otherwise. This Knowledge was needed at the dawn of Kaliyug. Vedas are laconic in form and hardly intelligible without interpretation. These books are products of man's contemplation and God's revelation. This Vedic religion gave three important things: Freedom of thought, Theory of Karma and concept of Pure Consciousness. By transcending one can experience this Consciousness [Brahman] which is root cause of all Creation. Various philosophies which came over a period of time have given their opinion on this Consciousness. Their interpretations at times seem different but all are unanimous in saying that absolute is ONE only. All say Creation is dependent on Absolute consciousness [Brahman].

All Creation is due to this Consciousness [Brahman]. This creation has separate existence but is dependent on Brahman. Advaitists labelled this creation as Mithya [Existence, which is Nonexistent in real sense]. This was labelled as Illusion by western writers which is wrong Interpretation. In fact there is no word in English language equivalent to Mithya. Philosophy at times looks abstruse but in essence it speaks of human mind. This philosophy does not allow dogmas, wants subject to experience himself nature of Truth [Brahman]. While west has been Probing outer world, Indian sages have been probing inner world to know Truth. Vedic Philosophy tells us Man is microcosm of GOD who is Macrocosm. Service to humanity is Service to GOD himself. Karma yoga and Bhakti yoga are forms for social action.

Hindu cosmology tells us how this world came into being [from nirgun Brahman to sagun Brahman]. Pantheism in Vedas is metaphorical representation of underlying forces which govern this Universe. Its time scale of cosmology is amazing [close to science]. Puranic stories were created to make subtle philosophy understandable to common man. Puranas are treasure house of history, give genealogy of kings who ruled ancient India. Puranas have acted as cover of fruit for Preserving Vedic wisdom and acted as its crutches which carried it till today.

Science and Mathematics originated in India and went to West via Iran and Arab world. Presence of Vedic deities in Zend Avesta is another proof of Vedic civilization influence in Persia. Dense network of "Tirths" and holy sites created sacred geography of India which helped in national Integration. Two great Epics have also played important role in national integration. These Epics have been rewritten and modified subject to times and local traditions. Mahabharata is true is proved by archeology and astronomical references. The position of Nav Graha mentioned in Mahabharata is fully validated by science.

This Vedic civilization spread from India to Europe via Iran long before Mesopotamia and Egyptian civilizations. It also spread in south East Asia [Thailand, Cambodia, Indonesia, Malaysia etc. ]. Bias of western world towards this civilization needs to be removed. It is duty of Indian scholars to shift name of India from foot notes of world history to main stream world history books.

Egyptian records tell us that they originally came from south, from a land called "Punt", an Asian country. Punt is believed to be Malabar coast of Deccan. There are writers like El Mansouri, Sir Jones, Paul Roberts Eramn who say migrants from India settled on banks of Nile.

Misinterpretation of Vedas done by Christian missionaries needs to be corrected. Historical material in Puranas and Vedas especially Rigveda needs to be analyzed and not ignored. Ancient dynasties who ruled Ancient India need to be given due place in history. Aryan invasion [1500BC] needs not only to be erased from history books but whole ancient Indian history needs to be rewritten. Historians all over write on the basis of written material available plus archeological finds. Why it being ignored in India's case? Why has n't Puranic stories, Epic narrative been used to compile Indian history? Indian ancient history is mystic not mythical. Vedas are records of ancient spiritual teaching of humanity. Vedas and Puranas give us details of Bharatvarsha, its people and their beliefs.

It is really sad that Indian universities still have western history books and western translations of Vedas on shelves. Acceptance of this western interpretation of Vedas amounts to self-Betrayal. A history written with particular set of mind is no history.

Tolerance does not mean to accept false and distorted views. Indian intellectuals need to rise, correct the wrong doings and put Indian history at proper place. Keeping Indian history in foot notes will be injustice to India and its people. India, mystical country has been invaded so many times but has managed to preserve evidence of its civilization till today. It is our duty to carry it forwards.

Hinduism in West is reflected through lens of Abrahamic religions thus theological uniqueness of Hinduism is totally being compromised. One has to read Vedas on their own terms and not from perspective of other religions. Indian culture is a mix of spirituality and materialism, a point missed by West. Rigveda is not just a history book. It is a book on human mind. Puranas give us traditional history.

It is saddening to note that modern Indian scholars are not coming up with realistic version of history of ancient India.

Humboldt------"Bhagavad-Gita is perhaps the loftiest and the deepest thing that world has to show".

# BIBLIOGRAPHY

1. The Story of Civilization: Our Oriental Heritage – By Will Durant.
2. The Invasion That Never Was - By Michel Danino and Sujata Nahar p. 26.
3. Pargiter FC 1972--Ancient Indian historical tradition. Delhi [Moti lal banarsi dass.
4. Maurice Winternitz- A history of Vedic literature, vol 1, p277, 2010.
5. MacDonnell 1900: A history of Sanskrit literature.
6. Rendell HR, Dennell RW, Halim M 1989, Paleolithic and Pleistocene investigations in Soan valley, north Pakistan, British archaeological reports in international series, Cambridge University press.
7. Jarrige c, JF Jarrige, RH Meadow and G. Quivron 1995, Mehargarh field reports 1975—1985—From Neolithic to Indus valley civilization Deptt of culture and tourism, Govt of Sindh and ministry of foreign affairs, France.
8. Kenoyer, J Mark 1988 the ancient cities of Indus valley civilization, Oxford University press.
9. Concise history of the world, an illustrated time line, The National Geographic.
10. Aryabhata---Famous mathematician. Enwikipedia. org/wiki/aryabhata. www. famous.
11. Racial Elements in the population by Dr. B. S. Guha
12. Srikanth Talageri----Aryan invasion theory---a Reappraisal.
13. South East Asia stone age, Wikipedia org/wiki/southeast Asia stone age.
14. Induscivilization/encyclopediaBritannica. www. britannica. com/topic/indus civilization.
15. Indus valley civilization Wwwssnet. ucla. edu/indu, university of California.
16. V Aggarwal: decodehindumythology. blogspot. com/Krishna.
17. Origins of Vedic civilization—Sanskrit texts and Stotras, Kenneth Chandler.
 Sanskrit. safire. com/pdf/origins.

18 S. P Gupta, - Indus Sara swat civilization: origin, people, and issues, 1996, p160-161.

19. Lal, B. B- The earliest civilization of South Asia, 1997, p162.

20. Kak Subash-Astronomical code of Rigveda 1994.

21. Rig Vedic India by A C Das, university of Calcutta, 1921

22 [http://quatr. us/maps/indoeuropean. htm]

23. Ibdi 22.

24Scientific Verification of Vedic Knowledge: Archaeology Online by David Osborn

25 Sarasvati, the lost river-by Michael Danino

26Ibid. 25

27. Solar dynasty: enwikipedia. org/wiki/suryavansha.

28. Indian monarchs--enwikipedia. org/wiki/list of Indian monarchs.

29.Vartak

http/www.hindunet.org/hinduhistory/ancient/Mahabharata.

30. Professor Achar BN: "Date of Mahabharata war on simulations using planetarium software" Ed—Suryakanth U kamath

Bangalore, India, 2004, p65-115]

31. Ibid. [4]

32. Ibid. [5]

33. Sanderson Beck-- "Literature of India"

34. Ibid. [30]

35. Sahoo etal 2006: A Prehistory of Indian Y chromosome: evaluating demi diffusion scenario. Proceedings of national academy of sciences 103 [4], 843-8. ]

36. Ibid. 35.

37. Arya 1 -by Anjani Pandey, Vivekananda Kendra Patrika 1 Aryan Invasion Theory Vol. 40 ]

38. Ibid. 17.

39. American heritage dictionary of the English language. Ed William Morris [Boston and New York]: Houghton Miftlin1969,

article by Calvin Watkins pxix. \

40. Professor Renfrew of Cambridge—"-Indo-Europeans in India as early as 6000BC".

41. Professor Schaffer--"Rigveda initially Sarasvati based, Indus civilization 2600BC—1900BC. "

42. Ibid. 18, 19

43. Burrow T--A cultural history of India, Clarendon press oxford 1975 p21.

44. Lunar dynasty—enwikipedia. org/wiki/lunar dynasty.

45. Kenoyer JM----"Birth of a civilization", Archeology, Jan/feb 1998, 52-56, p61

46. Kenneth Kennedy: "Have Aryans been identified in the prehistoric skeletal record of South Asia?" in georgeErdosy. Ed: TheIndo-Aryans of ancient south Asia, p49-54 1995.

47. Rajaram NS-- Hindustan times, Aryan invasion of India. The myth and truth 2000, April8

48. Frawley David---The Rigveda and history of India.

49. Ibid. 4, 31.

50. B. G. Tilak, The Orion, or research into antiquity of Vedas, Bombay 1893.

51. Ibid. 48

52. 16 mahajanpadas—ancient history of India. www. you tube. com.

53. Ibid. 45

54. Maurice Winternitz---A history of vedic literature, v1, p277, 2010.

55. Ibid. 7

56 Distortions in indian history—Rama Krishna rao.

57. Ibid. 50

58. Dharampal. -INDIA-Science and technology in the 18th century, Impex, India, 1971 p9-69.

59. Kivisild etal 2003: The genetic heritage of earliest settlers persist both in Indian tribal and caste populations. Am, J HumGenet. feb72 [2], 313-32.

60. Dr P. Priyadarshi: History of ancient India---over one lac years.

61. Ibid. 46

62. Ibid. 60

63. Ibid. 59

64. Sahoo et al 2006: A prehistory of Indian Y chromosome: Evaluating demi diffusion scenario. Proceedings of national academy of sciences 103 [4], 843--8.

65. Kantanen etal 2009, Maternal and paternal genealogy of Eurasian taurine cattle www. nature. com. Journal home Achieves.

Original article.

66. Underhill etal 2009: Haplo group R-M17. Enwikipedia. org/wiki/haplo

67. Michel Danino:" Genetics and Aryan debate-on line". Archeology on line. net/artifacts/genetics.

68. Quintana-Murci: "Where west meets East: The complex DNA landscape of the south west and central Asian corridor. American. J. of Human genetics 74 [5]: 827-45, May 2004
.

69. V Macaulay, Hill, Achill etal: "Single rapid coastal settlement of Asia revealed by analysis of complete mitochondrial genomes". Science 13, May 2005, V308, N 5724 PP1034-36.

70. Oppenheimer S---The real Eve: Modern man's journey out of Africa. 2003 Carrol and Graff publication, New York.

71. W F Allman, "Eve explained: How ancient humans spread across Earth". Website of discovery channel 21 Aug 2014. ]

72. Ibid 70.

73. Michel Danino:" Genetics and Aryan debate-on line". Archaeology on line. net/artefacts/genetics.

74. Witzel M 1995: Early Sanskritization, origin and development of Kuru state. Pdf electronic. J. of Vedic studies 14, 1995.

75. Ibid, 54.

76. Mahajanapadas, en. wikipedia. org/wiki/Mahajanapadas.

77. Mahajanapadas: www. newworldencyclopedia. org/entry/mahajanpada.

78. Ibid 74.

79. Kosala kingdom—enwikipedia. org/wiki/kosala kingdom.

80. P. Bhatnagar: "Dating of Rama era". Bharat gyan— Historical Rama by Hari.

81. Ibid. 30

82. Lal B—The earliest civilization of SouthAsia, p162, 1997.

83. Ibid. 33.

84. Solar Dynasty---enwikipedia. org/wiki/ suryavansha.

85. Ibid. 48, 51.

86. Jayaram v -"- History, antiquity and chronology of Hinduism".

87. India's contribution to world---www. you tube. com/watch.

http/en. wikipedia. org/wiki/list of indian inventions and discoveries.

.

88. Most powerful ancient indian sages/incredible india, 5 great scientists of ancient india.
http/www. youtube. com/watch
89. Maurice's history vol 111, p 104.
90. Sir w. Jones, in Asiatic research v 11, p40.

**Additional literature cited:**

. Rajaram NS and David Frawley: ". -Vedic Aryans and the origins of civilization". 2nd edition New Delhi. Voice of India 1997.
. Feuerstein, George, Subhash kak and David Frawley
. "In search of the cradle of civilization". Quest books:Wheaton111 1995
. Frawley D: The myth of Aryan invasion of India. Voice of India, New Delhi 1994.
. Majumdar RC---History and culture of Indian people. The Vedic age V1.
. R S Chaurasia: History of ancient India: Earliest times to 1000AD.
. Ancient India-kings. blogspot. com
. Kulke, Rothermund etal 1998: a history of India ISBN978-0-415-32920-0.
. Basham AL 2008: The wonder that was India: History and culture of Indian subcontinent before coming of Muslims ISBN 978-1-59740-5997.
. Majumdar 2001: "Ethnic population of India as seen from evolutionary perspective". J. BIOSCI, 26 [usuppl]:533-544.
. Mountain JL, Herbert JM, etal1995: Demographic history of India and mtDNA sequence diversity.
. India's contribution to world: Arjuna sayanim and Rajiv Dixit.
. Upinder Singh 2008: A history of ancient and early medieval India: From Stone Age to 12th century Pears on education, India
. Misra VS 2007: Ancient Indian dynasties, Bhartiya vidya bhavan. .

. Raju 1997: The philosophical traditions of India. Motilal banarsi das publication, New Delhi.

. Gupta and Ramachandran 1976: Mahabharata:" Myth or reality". Agam prakasham, New Delhi.

. Subash Kak 2000: "-On the chronological frame work for Indian culture". Indian council of philosophical research.

. PusalkarAD---History and culture of Indian people, . V1, chapter xiv p273.

. Hindu time line veda. wikidot. com/Hindu-time line.

. Rajaram NS: Aryan invasion: History or Politics? Hindu website. com/history/Aryan invasion.

. Rao SR: " Lothal and Indus valley civilization", Asia publishing house Bombay, India, 1973.

 Sandersonbeck: VedasandUpanishads. www. san. beck. org/Ec7- Vedas.

Vedic/Indian civilization---The most advanced, oldest and continuous.

U. tube. enwikipedia. org/wiki/vedas.

Harry old meadow 2007---Light from East:Eastern wisdom for modern West.

Ram Setu---An engineering marvel of5076BC

www. youtube. com/watch.

Balathal, Rajasthan---enwikipedia. org/wiki/balathal.

Sengupta 1947—"Ancient Indian chronology", Calcutta university.

Flood, Gavind 1996: An introduction to Hinduism p164—167, Cambridge university press.

ISBNo-521-43878-0.

Roy Chaudhuri H 1972---Political history of ancient India, Calcutta, university of Calcutta.

-The puzzle of origins, New research in the history of mathematics and ecology by N. S. Rajaram.

Historic Rama by Nilesh Nilkanth Oak.

When did Mahabharata happen? by Nilesh Nilkanth Oak.

--From authorsHindu superiority: An attempt to determine the position of Hindu race in the scale of nations. 3rd edition 1922.

--Bharatvarsha-The cradle of civilizations—Sham Misri.

# AUTHORS

## Dr. M. L. Babu

I was borne and brought up in Kashmir. I lived in Kashmir till my migration from valley in 1990. I now belong to community which not only is scattered all-over globe but is endangered too.

My interests besides my profession are in ancient of India and Vedas. I have travelled a lot and interacted with various people. I have perused various religious books. I have come to conclusions that India's past is hidden in Puranic stories. My professional articles stand published in both national and international journals. Now I am concentrating on my passion, Puranic stories and their relevance today. I have written on Hindu philosophy, God/religion, Hindu beliefs and rituals.

## Sham S Misri

I was born, brought up, educated, lived and married in Kashmir. Did master's degree in science and joined as lecture, later shifted to central services and retired from same organization as a senior level officer.

We were forced to migrate out of Kashmir in 1990. I along with my wife and children have widely travelled to various countries like, USA, UK, and Canada etc. Now I live at Seattle with my children.

There are many publications in various scientific journals and magazine by me. My passion is reading and writing. Author has written on Shaivism, Hindu gods, history and on many other topics.

## Kusum Babu

I was born, brought up in Kashmir. I did my master's in education from Kashmir University. I joined education deptt of state. My interest lies in literature, History and religious philosophy. Now I have resorted to writing for youngsters of India to make them aware of glorious past.

Made in the USA
Las Vegas, NV
17 September 2021